Melanie Silgardo was born in Bombay and lived there until 1984. She graduated from the University of Bombay, and set up a poetry publishing co-op, Newground, in 1977. For two years she was editor of Macmillan India's Bombay branch. A selection of her poetry, *The Earthworm's Story,* was published in *Three Poets* (Newground, 1978), and *Skies of Design,* a solo volume was nominated the best first volume of poetry from Asia for the Commonwealth Poetry Prize 1986. She has lived in London since 1984, and is an editor at Virago Press.

Janet Beck was born in 1964 in Lancashire and studied Drama and English at the University of Hull. She is a writer and teacher and now lives and works in London. In 1987, she helped set up the Women's Theatre Workshop with Cheryl Robson. They co-edited *The Women Writer's Handbook* (Aurora Metro, 1990) and contributed to *Taking Reality by Surprise* (Women's Press, 1991). Her play *My Michelle* was developed and performed as part of The Soho Poly Theatre's Blueprints scheme and she has had poems and short stories published.

virago
new
poets

edited by **melanie silgardo**
and **janet beck**

Published by VIRAGO PRESS Limited, June 1993
20-23 Mandela Street, Camden Town, London NW1 0HQ

A CIP catalogue record for this title
is available from the British Library

Printed in Great Britain

Contents

Editors' Note

For us, bringing this anthology together has been a hugely rewarding experience. We received a mass of responses to notices we'd put out, calling for work from poets who had not yet had their work published in individual volumes. The process of selection was a difficult one, but it was ruled by one main criterion: excellence. We were not looking for particular themes; we were seeking to present poetry by women that transcended all the narrow definitions and expectations.

We discovered what we already knew was there: poems that dazzle, poems that contemplate, poems that subvert – the raw energy of Androula Savvas Pistolas' 'Maureen Is a Funny Girl', the full-bodied and sensual imagery of Margaret Browne's 'Landscape', the dark and sinister undertones of T.P. Tolkien's 'About the Lady Who Married Colonel Packard', the precision of Wendy Ruthroff 'To Fisher, Almost Blind At Eight', the spiky terror of Maureen Hanafan's 'Bogeyman'. These are only a few, but all communicate a richness and complexity of experience.

We would like to thank Virago Press for making this anthology possible, and for leaving the landscape of possibilities wide open for us to explore; Michèle Roberts for affirming our faith in these poems; Jo Tracy for providing the link; and Kasha Dalal for uncomplaining help throughout. Not least, thanks to the poets in these pages for giving us the pleasure of their words.

Melanie Silgardo
Janet Beck
1993

Foreword

Michèle Roberts

As a teenager I wrote poems in secret. To protect the writing process I locked the bathroom door. To protect the poem against being read I copied it into a notebook which I hid in a drawer. Poetry was my private, solitary language, my true language, one I couldn't dream of uttering inside family life. Inner chaos and turbulence were my themes; sexual desire and sexual fear; violence. Classic adolescent stuff I suppose you could say. I was fervently Catholic, ridden with guilt about being female and unfeminine; writing poetry let me discover another self, one who was wild, decadent, free, rebellious, different, uncaring about unbelonging. Well, yearned to be, anyway.

In the sixth form four of us founded a Poetry Society, the one nun I loved and respected aiding and abetting us. We gave each other criticism and encouragement. We were writers, readers, publishers. We were an early prototype of the writers groups so important to me in my twenties. We gave each other permission to stray from the binary opposites of femininity offered at the time: ugly swot versus boy-mad thicko. Writing poetry that was comic, satiric and savage, we simultaneously created selves who were messier, bitter and more awkward than the stereotypes.

Many people writing poetry during adolescence, then stop, perhaps under the pressure of becoming what the world calls grown-up: no more play and irrationality; get out there and stop wasting time and earn a living. Poetry may re-surface at times of crisis, like falling in love or mourning a death, when the rational self cracks open the unconscious erupts and with it the need to write. Poetry in emergency, not as part of life. There is terrific subtle pressure on people to stop writing it. It withers and dies and stays in the drawer as a memory, dry leaves.

To resist that pressure, to keep on writing, you need a certain amount of selfishness and bloodymindedness. My strategy was to parade as a misfit, an eccentric, at the psychic cost of feeling that perhaps the family was right and I *was* mad. But what helped me greatly, I'm convinced, looking back, was that group of friends who egged each other on to write and helped create a space in which it could happen. No accident, surely, that I went on making that occur over and over again. Being in a writers group brought the immense practical benefits of learning how to improve, how to re-draft with endless patience, how to appreciate work utterly different from one's own; it also symbolised clearing a space in the imagination into which poems could come. Out of those early groups in the seventies came several anthologies of poems which we published ourselves and sold ourselves. Then, the feminist presses, at least, began to take us seriously as poets, even if the poetry establishment took a little longer and still has trouble, sometimes, reading work that's involved with gender in some way. We helped to create a counter-culture friendly to poetry and were in turn nourished by it.

What I notice nowadays is how many women there are writing and publishing poetry. It's good if you don't have to feel like a pioneer all the time but can just get on with your work without feeling like a representative (better than feeling like a monster perhaps). Each new generation of poets breaks the ground in their own way. This can involve discarding feminine/feminist aesthetics, or taking them for granted, or building on them. There are more spaces for writing poetry today, I think: more poetry groups, classes, residential courses, local workshops. It's more normal to be a woman and a poet than it used to be, and the reading/listening public can enjoy a range and variety of poetic voices if they know where to look.

What struck me, on first looking through this volume, was how many of these poets I had already heard of and read. They are certainly not beginners in any simple sense, most of them, but have been energetically pushing their work out for some time. They are 'new poets' in that they haven't published solo volumes, yet clearly they operate within and benefit from existing poets' networks or have helped create new ones: I've discovered their work through public readings I've been to, workshops I've attended or taught, magazines and anthologies I've read. The second thing that struck me about this collection was the poems' confidence of tone and subject-matter, their lack of apology or defensiveness, their willingness to pick up stifling ideologies (feminist ones included) and peer at what lurks underneath. Poetry, by its metaphorical nature, is subversive of simple truths, and many of the poems included here testify to that. The ones I like best not only display a love of language and craft but mix odd, new insights with warmth and passion. Reading the entire volume straight through at a single gulp gave me great pleasure. So did going back and browsing. Now I think how good it would be to be able to find more work by my favourites amongst these poets.

The main outlet for poets at the start of their careers remains anthologies like this one. Anthologies are all the rage in these recessionary times. Safer, less risky, I suppose. They ought to operate as springboards to solo collections, but it's very hard to make that happen. Poetry lists are being severely cut back. It's difficult even for 'established' poets to find a publisher these days.

The answer is not to give up; to keep going. I wish all the poets represented in this groundbreaking volume all the selfishness and bloody-mindedness they need to survive and to flourish. The sense of community, fragile and stroppy and affectionate is, I think, already there.

1993

MONIZA ALVI

MONIZA ALVI was born in Pakistan in 1954 and now teaches
in London. She is also co-editor of *Poetry London Newsletter*.
In 1991, she was joint winner of the Poetry Business
Competition. A pamphlet collection with Peter Daniels was
published by Smith/Doorstop in 1992 and her first
collection is due from Oxford University Press in late 1993.

'The Country at my Shoulder' was a prizewinner in the
1991 Cardiff International Poetry Competition. 'I Would
Like to be a Dot in a Painting by Miro' was published in
the *London Review of Books*. 'On Finding a Letter to Mrs
Vickers on the Pennine Way' appeared in *Poetry Review*.

THE COUNTRY AT MY SHOULDER

There's a country at my shoulder,
growing larger – soon it will burst,
rivers will spill out, run down my chest.

My cousin Azam wants visitors to play
ludo with him all the time.
He learns English in a class of seventy.

And I must stand to attention
with the country at my shoulder.
There's an execution in the square –

The women's dupattas are wet with tears.
The offices have closed
for the white-hot afternoon.

But the women stone-breakers chip away
at boulders, dirt on their bright hems.
They await the men and the trucks.

I try to shake the dust from the country,
smooth it with my hands.
I watch Indian films –

Everyone is very unhappy,
or very happy,
dancing garlanded through parks.

I hear of bribery, family quarrels,
travellers' tales – the stars
are so low you think you can touch them.

Uncle Aqbar drives down the mountain
to arrange his daughter's marriage.
She's studying Christina Rossetti.

When the country bursts, we'll meet.
Uncle Kamil shot a tiger,
it hung over the wardrobe, its jaws

Fixed in a roar – I wanted to hide
its head in a towel.
The country has become my body –

I can't break bits off.
The men go home in loose cotton clothes.
In the square there are those who beg –

And those who beg for mercy.
Azam passes the sweetshop,
names the sugar monuments Taj Mahal.

I water the country with English rain,
cover it with English words.
Soon it will burst, or fall like a meteor.

I WOULD LIKE TO BE A DOT IN A PAINTING BY MIRO

I would like to be a dot in a painting by Miro.

Barely distinguishable from other dots,
it's true, but quite uniquely placed.
And from my dark centre

I'd survey the beauty of the linescape
and wonder – would it be worthwhile
to roll myself towards the lemon stripe,

Centrally poised, and push my curves
against its edge, to get myself
a little extra attention?

But it's fine where I am.
I'll never make out what's going on
around me, and that's the joy of it.

The fact that I'm not a perfect circle
makes me more interesting in this world.
People will stare forever –

Even the most unemotional get excited.
So here I am, on the edge of animation,
a dream, a dance, a fantastic construction,

A child's adventure.
And nothing in this tawny sky
can get too close. Or move too far away.

ON FINDING A LETTER TO MRS VICKERS
ON THE PENNINE WAY

A bird with a torn tail hops under ferns
and points its beak to the wall.

A letter to Mrs Vickers is trodden into the path –
colours have run into edges soft as cotton.

Mrs Vickers, Mrs Vickers
you have won, you have almost won
a Ford Escort. We of the Prizes Department
are sending you a draft of the Award Certificate.

Earth trickles over it like a child's pattern.

Mrs Vickers, calling your number at Stoneway
we would like to tell you
you're in with a winning chance.
Don't miss the cellophane window.

It shines like a dirty film of ice.

Mrs Vickers, don't forget to tell us
all about yourself.
Then tread this well into the path
where the mossy fronds dart like fishes –

And the bird fans out its broken tail.

ANGELA BROWN

ANGELA BROWN is a Creative Writing tutor and poet included in *Taking Reality By Surprise* and *In the Gold of the Flesh* (Women's Press, 1990). She is currently settling down to family life in north-west England.

CAP O'RUSHES*

One

I love you as fresh meat loves salt.
You love me like maggots. Door's shut in my face.
Would you leave your best treasure without a vault?

Additions to linen was my worst fault,
and refusing to play any creep-mouse chase.
I love you as fresh meat loves salt.

Well, what if to romping I called a halt?
My wit and womanhood's mine: no disgrace.
Would you leave your best treasure without a vault?

Grown folk can roister on milk and malt
and wit. They don't need wine and lace.
I love you as fresh meat loves salt.

You've drunk; fen's got your head by default.
The fog from your piss is now all my embrace.
Would you leave your best treasure without a vault?

I prized you for granite; you're gloopy gault.
You dangered my spaces. I grasp for grace.
I love you as fresh meat loves salt.
Would you leave your best treasure without a vault?

* Cap O'Rushes is a kind of English Cinderella from Suffolk. The folk tale may have been the inspiration for *King Lear*, it is believed.

CAP O'RUSHES

Two

We used to gather rushes together,
Eleanor, Ann and I –
Master's daughters, pretty and clever.
Eleanor, Ann and none

That taught me to plait the withy and reed,
Eleanor, Ann and I –
That warned me, 'Play, but mind you don't bleed'
Eleanor, Ann and none

Lindsey-woolsey, linen and silk,
Eleanor, Ann and I –
Over the curves that grew with the milk.
Eleanor, Ann and none

Workmaids sing if they get enough bread,
Eleanor, Ann and I –
Sisters sing over spoils, now I'm dead.
Eleanor, Ann and none

Three to make plait and two to make twine,
Eleanor, Ann and I –
One to make nothing, in reeds dressed fine.
Eleanor, Ann and none

He loves me, he loves me not, we'd play,
Eleanor, Ann and I.
Rush whispers treachery. I'll away.
Eleanor, Ann and none

CAP O'RUSHES

Nine

Pools have bounds, for all that reeds confuse.
Roads have ways to go, most lanes
reach places. Trees grip into squelch
and found a footing, kingly, queenly.

Father's incontinent mouth let sauces
ooze to crust his beard. Even sheared
sheep still have skins. I make a cap
o'rushes, fashion hurdles – and gates!

YOU/STOCK

For the makers of the Mosaic at Stepping Hill Outpatients

Yield as tired tile. Be fragment. Chip
Out, shape self. Group. Bond safe. Make
Unique from useless. Be gem from junk.

Stop. Breathe. Allow your heart to
Ford the flooding, impossible rivers. Grab

One mirrored glimpse of yourself. Still smile.
Round range, up challenging banks. A dwelling awaits.
Hill, hail, heat, humidity? Revel in elements!

Stock yourself in any image here. Load a narrow boat of dreams:
port you will, safely, your best self a precious cargo.

Yes, you can shift and span. Names change. Places make
Or unmake themselves. Select. Self-mosaic merrily!
Uphill, stepping steadily, you can arrive, survive!

CACKHANDED

Imelda Connelly,
Why must you drop everything?
Imelda Connelly,
You trip on your shadow!
Imelda Connelly,
Stop hashing with scissors,
Imelda Connelly,
You're clumsy and bad–oh!
  I created the magic tale
    For my group's play
      To win the prize.

Imelda Connelly,
Good girls fold their clothing.
Imelda Connelly,
Why won't you be neat?
Imelda Connelly,
Your writing's appalling!
Imelda Connelly –
The worst in our street.
  Their gerbil nearly bored to death
    Till I improvised
      Some toys.

Imelda Connelly,
Did nobody tell you
The world wants girls
Who do everything tidy.
Imelda Connelly,
Did nobody tell you –
Messers don't get to be
Any man's bride-y?
  Does nobody notice that I'm left-handed?
  Funny that they don't understand it.

TRUE SCIENCE

It all went still in the Mobile.
The Practical bit kept Tan and I busy
with noting, recording, predicting if feathers
or peas in the scale-pan would make it come equal.
Miss opened the window to stop us from baking
and breeze made our feathers float under the desks.
There was scraping of chairs and Tan's giggles
and Christopher trying to tickle us down at the floor;
there were peas pinging, pans clanking, Miss fussing David
to tabulate findings and wait for each balance –
then, somehow, while scales hovered
breeze held its breath and I saw that
our findings had pattern, and Dave
and the others got poise with their beams
then results that made sense-
                    and the whole hut held quiet.

Margaret Browne

MARGARET BROWNE was born in Birkenhead and now lives in
Kent. Her poetry has appeared in journals in Canada and
America and in anthologies. She won a Prose Prize and a
South East Arts Literary Group Prize in 1990.

LANDSCAPE

Our cousin talked of old times,
childhood in California, the granary loft –
gossamer memories, full of sun.
In particular she spoke of apples,
Red Astrachans from Russia,
Aunt Dorcas, Seek-no-Further,
crimson cheeked Maiden's Blush.

We saw the cool green galleries,
meditated on the soft rains of spring.

The need for a cold cellar entered
into our calculations,
most apples coming in the fall.
Flavour we took into account
texture, white crispness, juiciness,
mellow flesh cooked with quince,
wood smoke winding on the wind –
summer's lush promise becoming
autumn's fulfillment.
Windfalls, leaves sloughed to earth.

When she left we brooded
counting Jonathans, Winesaps instead of sheep.
The trees blossomed, strong arms lifted high
above counterflow of rippling fescues, timothy grass.
The orchard grew in our minds,
not in the dark grained soil.
Apples have that way with dreamers.

SAUSALITO

Bearing salt on her breath,
the wind runs in soft darkness.
Sailors who had been elbow deep in
bone and blubber, fierce hunters
taking life with easy conscience,
unloaded full casks upon this shore,
poaching the sea's cornucopia, whales –
those great Leviathans from Siberia.

Every man, mahogany-hued, a gladiator.
Stormy waters taking their secrets,
weaknesses, on the lip of a wave,
folding them, fish-lined fathoms deep
in silk evergreen closets –
mariners who watched sea unicorns bask
and respected the albatross legend.

Then the New World was young, no auditor
calculated the score, no-one knew
the rich oboe music of the ocean.
A cruel harpoon thrust ended life,
roiled waters, vermilion stained, spreading,
a cacophony of winged scavengers
tearing the whale's barnacled hide.

Now, early in a cool Sausalito morning,
sun smiles down on clapboard houses,
yachts, stark white, pack the marina
parked neatly as waiting cars, houseboats wake.
The ancient seafaring ghosts have fled,
a last whaler sighs in gentle swells
as blithe tourists inspect her decks.
Beyond the bay, fog moves in closer.

LAMMASTIDE

Lammastide –
the last barbecue.

Crab apples
heretic red
fall at first wind,
bruise-thumbed.

Two magpies,
Punch and Judy,
swazzle-throated at dusk.
A Moselle sky.

Laughter persimmon sharp,
lantern light, guitars searching
for the right tune,
voices fade – enigmatic.

Weightless,
ghost of the hop tallyman wanders
forever reckoning
bines and bushels,
bushels and bines.

Owl,
night's incubus drifts,
the horses know his step
restless, nudging in hot shadows
they feel him in the bone.

The amber beads of summer
have slipped through time's fingers,
an abacus counted – told.

JILL DAWSON

JILL DAWSON has published widely and in 1992 was the
major Eric Gregory Award winner for poetry. She is the
editor of *The Virago Book of Wicked Verse*. A Northerner, she
now lives in Hackney with her partner and their young son.

'Pregnant Woman Speaks to the Sea' and 'The Crossing'
were first published in *In the Gold of the Flesh* (ed. Rosemary
Palmeira, Women's Press, 1990); 'Escape to Shanghai' in
Writing Women (Vol 5 No 2, 1986); and 'Sweetbite Air' in
Slow Dancer (No 28, Nov 1992).

PREGNANT WOMAN SPEAKS TO THE SEA

she says:

come, sea
make a cave of me
hollow me
like this slim blue shell
empty me
like this broken egg
dropped cold and round
on these rocks
return me
to myself
like the tides
come, sea
make a shell of me
free me
wash me

SWEETBITE AIR

In my mother's spare bedroom
under a wild, conspiring sky,
he asks me if anyone ever loved me
like this. I tell him, honestly,
that no one ever did. There is

a pause,
filled with scrambled breathing
and the beating of a watchful moon.
It isn't even a full moon.
Not the heady violet sort
which no doubt lit the sand
while the woman he loves
clung to his salty body,
his promise of her future.

Landy. I am not glittering midnight
coconut palms. I am not clear rain
from the mountains. I am not
the sweetbite air
you have often described to me.
After everything, centuries,
must we have love now, too?
Clasping you, in my honeyed
fearful shell, what can I offer
but a net of winter mornings,
the shivered dreams
of a cowardly, longing girl.

ESCAPE TO SHANGHAI

These mornings
when I'm left alone
I've taken to watching
Breakfast TV.
The Queen is in China
I watch her dumpy yellow
dress and hat
make its way to Shanghai's
Famous Tea House.
There she will take
four types of tea
(while I sip the milky
coffee my sister suggested
to keep my strength up.
I have not been eating lately).
The Queen has come five full
circles of the Zodiac.
This means she is very mature.
I have come exactly two.
This means I am not.
I'm round at my sister's, watching telly.
I would like to phone my home
to see if anyone is in
but last night I threw my phone
at the wall
and broke it.

The Queen's tea is picked by virgins.
My coffee no doubt exploits
peasants in Nicaragua.
I drink it anyway.

Is the Queen going to try her hand
at chopsticks?
Who gives a toss?

They make the streets
zig zag shaped in Shanghai
because evil spirits move in straight lines.

I think I need to go there.

THE CROSSING

All night the sea tossed me
like egg yolk in a basin
and rocked the baby
in my belly

so here, arriving
it is not I, but we
all churned up and frothing
with still, at the window
the sea of our crossing.

Milky, foaming
she laps at the door
while I'm lying in water
drowning, distraught

even in the bath
I'm assailed by kicks
the ugly hammering
of a hungry chick.

The wind and sea
puncture the fine membrane
of the house
while the child inside
rolls like an eyeball
beneath skin grown
fine as an eyelid.

JANE DRAYCOTT

JANE DRAYCOTT was born in 1954. She works as an English
teacher and as co-director of Four Corners Theatre
Company. She lives in Oxfordshire with her husband and
two young daughters. 'Braving The Dark' was shortlisted
for the 1992 Arvon Poetry Competition.

COSMONAUT 1992

The arcade scores his fifteenth orbit
of the earth today, and the silence on the radio
is crystal clear. Every two hours he passes
directly over his wife.

His body is on stand-by –
black tongues of hair break rank across his forehead
and his eyes are as dark and as deep as Lake Baikal,
absorbing all things.

At a more appropriate
moment, he will think of this as his sarcophagus.
Outside the portholes, there are more stars
than you could shake a stick at.

His mouth is set
with energy: the electrolyte of his saliva
has formed a battery between his tongue,
resting so long, and his teeth.

The earth and its oceans
are beautiful. He floats here like a baby for Unity, for Peace,
and his body is steeped in the aura
of regulation cleansing.

The power supply is unreliable
and condensation is a problem, but Progress is due,
bringing enough lunches and dinners to see him through
the next month.

He walks in the night
through the drift of his own waste which hugs the capsule.
His helmet fogs with his breathing. On the scales,
he is nothing.

He understands that Leningrad
is now St Petersburg, that living becomes harder by the day.
They will deliver him – he will search for the words,
he will appear unmoved.

WAR WIDOW

You are buried
In the weave of your old coat-sleeves
In the stitch of your old jumpers
And in the wood-pigeons' jungle at the bottom of the garden
In the last of dusk.

You are concealed
In the mesh of every morning,
Waiting to be discovered
Like the puzzle-book bird which hangs
upside down in the branches.

I try to concentrate
On the fixed lines: twigs, tiles and fences
Paving-stones and bricks,
The inlay of the humdrum.

But the air's weave is not so easy.
Shifting out of resolution, it insists
On pushing out your body at me:
Newsreel puppet living in the air,
A hologram in uniform.

Yesterday your ghost appearance,
Snapshot in a wartime feature, ambushed me:
My signals officer still giving out signals
After all these years.

And I knew your face
As if it were my own for me to look
Through into the camera.
Across the screen of dots I crept,
To infiltrate the ink and lie with you.

BRAVING THE DARK

in memory of my brother
Nigel P Draycott 1957–1988

and for the staff of London Lighthouse

I : Search

Passive, your glove allows me to enter
its five black-soft tunnels:
the tips however remain uninhabited,
your fingers having been longer than mine.

The words you typed and left, expecting to return,
file out across their electronic lawn.
I caress them with the cursor, like a medium
stroking the table at a seance.

At your pain on the answerphone tape my voice
sticks, as at the gaps in a linguaphone lesson
In tears, I sort the wafers of your clothes for friends —
straightjacketed in card you watch, and seem unmoved.

At last, day buckles and, awake in bed, I find you:
the deadweight limbs we turned two-hourly
and powdered to protect your baffled skin
become my own, crook'd flat along the sheet

and from the soft lame triangle that your mouth became
you breathe our childhood out upon my pillow.
Wearing the features of our father,
your frightened face sleeps inside mine.

II : Dream

The Vicar arrives by rowing-boat,
vampire-stalks our wet front path
and batlike settles out his cloak
for The Consolation of the Bereaved

(flashback to our mother's funeral
when we remarked how very like a piece of theatre
funerals are, as his hand webbed out
a fraction on his Book of Common Prayer).

His head is tortoising out to kiss me.
I am trying to explain my disinclination
to dance, when you appear suddenly from the lounge,
perfectly whole, to save me.

Outside the door the road is dry again
the vicar desubstantiated. At last
we're on our own and you can tell me
how it is that you're not really dead after all.

III : Piano-movers

They came like ambulance-men
in mufti, thick-soled
and trained to be careful.

Why then must he go in red blankets,
he had played it to know,
and the virus allowed to ride inside?

In one gentle tackle they had the legs
from under it. Winded, it blurted
strange harmonies and going down was still.

He had dreamt the last test
had come negative, though upon the keys
his Hansel-and-Gretel fingers unwove the fantastic lie.

Easing its deadweight
shoulder, they tucked the flung elbow flat
and pulled deftly on blankets and straps.

'Can't you change it?'
he'd asked of the strangers
who tended his body, but failed to reply.

Invisible neighbours watched its wheeled
passage, bumped prone down the front path
between unknown bearers.

IV : Mahogany

Pressing down in twos and threes
the slack teeth of the piano's smile
I try to conjure you,
your hip knuckling against mine
for just one more shambling duet.

You do not appear: I seal
the mute mahogany. Propped
on the music-rest I read
the notes you ink-embroidered
in a song for me: Lullay, and hush.

Scattered families of notes fragment
and shimmy above their own reflections.

It's a Lovely Day Tomorrow,
you used to sing
at gilt kosher soirees. Evening
lays out along the tautened strings:

the black silk thread
along the edge of your lapel
is as clear as your face
as in the dark you stand to sing
your heart out.

MARTINA EVANS

MARTINA EVANS was born in Cork in 1961 and lives and works in London as a radiographer. She is married with one baby daughter. Her poems have been published in *Poetry Ireland Review, New Irish Writing, The Rialto* and many other UK magazines. She was shortlisted for a Hennessey Cognac Award in 1992 and winner of the 1992 Frances Martin College Prize for Poetry Reading and Writing.

MY BROWN LACED SHOES

Where are my brown laced shoes?
In which I tramped Dean's fields and Greenhill road
And Island road, down Toureen past Danny O'Hanlon's,
Down the road from Burnfort school to run and lie flat
In the fairy ring with my satchel hurting my back.

Where are my brown laced shoes?
In which I ran from Jock the hee-hawing pony
Through the woods where every pine needle prick held
A scary fairy who might steal me away
If I was very lucky which I wasn't
In this world more full of weeping, I had an inkling

I did have an inkling indeed
Climbing up on to the lap of Old Mother Ireland,
A groaning Rosaleen,
A bitch who threw salt on my sadness.

Where are my brown laced shoes?
In which I cycled green Beech tunnels,
Trees woven over me, around me, under me,
Before me, behind me, beside me,
Choking the living daylights out of me.

Sent to listen to whiners you couldn't satisfy,
And nicer ones you wouldn't satisfy
Funerals, weddings, holy days of obligation
Many days of obligation when the best bonham hurled my books
And stuck pins in my inflatable dream coat.

They silenced me, smothered me, sickened me,
My dream coat held together with safety pins
I dry bawled silently into this world more full of weeping
As my brown laced shoes walked away, old and sad
Tapping quieter all the time.

THIS PASSION

I opened your wizard's jacket
with red and yellow stars,
loosened your face from
the green hood
your hands went wide like
the start of a blessing
and pulled, furious fingers
on my blouse, as I ached for
your touch, yet moved back.
Zipper quick was your hand
round my waist, taking
up the position, mouth caving
towards me.
Still brave, I shielded my body,
gasped, 'Take this!' as I put
the orange juice to your lips.

They call this passion, weaning.

BERTA FREIDSTADT

BERTA FREIDSTAT is a Londoner and has written poetry,
among other things, all her life. Her first poems about some
furry animals was published in the *Observer* in 1948. Since
then with some work on her style and content, she has been
published in several anthologies. She is co-editor of
Language of Water, Language of Fire (Oscars Press). She has
taught women creative writing for several years, and is
alternately depressed and awed by their talent and
commitment.

WOLVES

When it comes to the jugular
You really need
A woman for aim.
Pirahnas are comprehensive
But messy by comparison
And sharks are short sighted
Mainly
And have a terrible press
I suspect in fact
They could be affectionate
Given the right relationship
They have that rather glazed
Obsessive look
That you often see in the eye
Of long term couples.

When it comes to wolves
Research has shown
Them to be good parents
And monogamous
And all that stuff
About chasing sleighs

Across frozen wastes
Is the usual anthropomorphic
Misinterpretation.
A wolf of my acquaintance
A rather coy fellow
Once told me
That nothing could be further
From the truth than destruction
Au contraire he said he was French
Usually at the end of a long
Arctic or Russian winter
They'd all be so bored
With the same old songs
And anecdotes and faces
They were only seeking
To find fresh company
New friends who hadn't heard
Their jokes
And wolves love the balalaika.

And take octopuses
It's the same all over again
Home loving, shy
To the point of extinction
Totally misunderstood
Like dragons.

When it comes to the jugular
And cutting
Only a woman has the knowledge
Of where to stick the knife.

'I AM SNAKE'

I am snake
In winter hibernation
Straining for the sun
But it is only
Cleopatra's barge that passes
Alight
With beer and lanterns
And the sound of singing
And of slops being flung.

The barge lights wink
Across my scales
Until at last green
Diamonds
Turn blue.

My old friend the wasp
On her last legs
Is tired and sore
She longs for warmth
Or Death
And one last place
To lay her bitter sting
She says goodbye
As she flies low
Slowly after the sweetness
She can smell
From the party-boat long gone.

Then wake water
Rocks my nest
As damp creeps up
And soon will rot the straw
Soon
I will creep a little higher
A little dryer
And wait this long cold
Winter through.

In that white sky
Now I see the truth
Palely smiling at me
And in the silence
If I am still enough
I can hear the faint hoot
Of the old tug boat
At her winter mooring
Maybe she will stop here
Next spring.

'DOWN THE STEPS'

Down the steps
Of the pit I trod
Naked
As though to bathe
Only my ankles
Were cold
Perceiving as they did
New dirt
On my toes.
It was not a carpet
Across which I stepped
Something softer
Something decayed.
I lay down

By the body
Of my dying lover
Caressed
Her wrinkled breasts
Rejoicing
At this final reunion

> *My apologies & respect*
> *To all who were there*
> *I was not*
> *Your testimony*
> *Forms my imagination*

DIANA GITTINS

DIANA GITTINS writes poetry and non-fiction. She is the author of *The Fair Sex* and *The Family In Question* and has published poems in many different magazines.

'Listen to me, Henry Moore' was published in *Odyssey*, 1992.

LISTEN TO ME, HENRY MOORE

            There is a hole in me
                chiselled   lack
        men punch fists   through my gap
    children put heads in   relax
            I take it all   stare blankly to the sky
            am admired   yet nobody
                asks   why
            I ache this void

Once I lived solid in mud and slime
rain ran through my schisty veins
wilderness pillowed me
I supported terrain.

You cut me
turned me into
your vision
smoothed me, rounded me
set me on a pedestal
sold me – hole and all.

I tried to stuff my want with food
sucked fingers faecal with peanut butter
loaded my gutted washing machine
that drained to a
vacant drum.

I bathed in sex
quested men's tumescence
when the plug was pulled
my reward was a ring round
a hollow tub.

For a while my child
filled me
warm nowhere swelled to smiles
yet she grew her own
gap – left mine to cradle alone.

Still, now and then
wildness pervades me
hewn from earth to her I will topple, return
sweet ooze will make me whole again.

JOYOTI GRECH

JOYOTI GRECH was born in Dhaka, Bangladesh in 1963 and came to Britain at the age of eight. Her stories are published by Black Womantalk in their anthology, *Don't Ask Me Why,* and her poetry has appeared in *Artrage, Feminist Arts News, Bazaar* and *Inqilab* magazines. She has performed her work with Apples and Snakes, Asian Women Writers' Collective, on BBC Radio and with Arekopaneng South African Cultural Workers' Association.

FARAH'S FLIGHT

Farah flew out flew over
She was a little girl
    an old woman
    a young woman
at the centre of the world
with the blood jumping in her veins
and flesh still thick with muscles

Her arms are brown
her skin is warm, from the inside

Where she flew there was no madness
only a river and steady heat

There was thumping like the noise
a heart makes
    love
and breathing that was all
her own

Time passed, a drop
a spoonful,
a little electricity
She felt her face on
velvet grass she heard
glass/the air

Voices put a whisper in her ear and her eyes
saw

the night made it safe

Coming back took longer
along the way the moon was waiting
fat inside the black and
she knew
something/she didn't know/before

LOOKING FOR RIGOBERTA MENCHU IN THE CORRIDORS OF THE UN

I'm looking for Rigoberta Menchu in the UN building
running down these hollow halls and
checking every corner in
this place where states / rotate
the right for us to say
our little bit
just like states / deliberate
from time to time / their generosity to give
a little bit
back to us of what was
ours in the first place

– you're giving ME my land back?
– you're giving ME my words back?

So I'm looking for my sisters / fighting for
our right to speak
Rigoberta told me,
Sometimes we speak too loud for them / they try to
shut the door but
we just turn around and come right through the back

and I'm thinking
Yes /
Rigoberta / your people and mine
should get together pretty soon

but in the meantime / we're wading through
the rippling ribbons of red tape and
Naw Louisa in the lobby room
reveals to me the story of
her Karen people
she tells me how
they crossed the shifting sands
to reach the fertile lands in
Burma / in Thailand / and all through
South East Asia
– We're everywhere / she tells me in
her Southern California voice

and I want to hug her in
our shared excitement / You know,
Louisa / your people and mine
should get together pretty soon

Just like Bernadette McAliskey / was saying
from her crossing over
that short strip of sea that keeps
her island separate but colonised by
the one we're standing on now

– ancient & timeless / sacred & secular
– the shifting sands of standing-strong resistance

because

We are a People in Struggle ours is a Culture of Change

& there are so many of us / so solid / so sure & so I know
that when I find
Rigoberta Menchu in this UN building
were going to make
some / strong / new
United
Nation.

MAUREEN HANAFAN

MAUREEN HANAFAN was born in November 1956, the fifth
of nine children. Her background is working class, Roman
Catholic. She has no educational attainments. She is blessed
with the pleasures (and pain) of a very extended family
which includes two daughters of her own, Lucy and Maisie.
She lives with her husband Bill and children in Hemel
Hempstead. This is her first published work.

LUCY

My soft beige cats face
rendered down, found
then lost again
in purrs of sticky kitty fat
(impermanent domestic flab
for shifting to and fro)

Novitiate
a chubby nun
wimpled in my untrained arms –
across the bed,
9 child wise,
a woman said
'you are a cow
handling a shilling'

Dollies don't
suck sick shit sleep
your blind instinctive ways disgust me –
the whole milky ward disgusts me
the soft soled squish of expert midwives
the guilty flush of blood

Forgive me mother
for I am tender
oh I am so tender,
inarticulate

(postscript:
each glistening kiss
a snotty pearl
that treasured trove
I never hoped to find
love does exist in these –
and other pretty tyrannies)

BOGEYMAN

Gathering dust
a mossy old man in a suit
on a hill,
he pulls and
he peeps
a silly threnody
intoned on the
bone of an
ossified tongue –
'sweet meat your purple
        feverish kiss
is plush to my tongue
        as warm hippocras,
Cocker up Cocker up
repression and rage'.

To the child he is a teacher
a rearing snatching hobbyhorse
swirled in skirt and board –
a ginger fart left
hanging in a sniggered class.

To the child he is a priest
a tickling sniff of ginger snuff
well oiled with extreme unction –
dogmata pock his face
where eyes should see
and I cannot get free –

Phallic as hatpins,
an icepick of distaste,
I enter him –
to MY tongue he is canker,
a flyblown skull whipped
white as albumen –

I CAN NOT GET FREE
carvings in lard
his unused hands
enfinger me –
Cocker up Cocker up
old Cock on Calvary

SUFFER IN SILENCE

I roar awake
beside a plastic cot
I wear a gown, back to front,
my bum is cold
I beat the air (I leave my breast to others)
odd how we learn to swat our hurt like flies

This morning unaware
dishabille in the salty duvet
I caught drowsy Justice

mirrored in the wardrobe door
unbalanced (avoids the fibbing scale)
fumbling out twin totems of her
    RIGHT TO BE HERE –
red shaped wax and wadded wool
(a rusty whiff of ancient blood
like tardy cat food impolitely hints)

Between nappy changes
I read my book
Emily is dead and Anne is dying
she reaches out and Charlotte sighs
'take courage sister' –
beyond the looking glass
supine Justice lifts a leg and groans
'take courage sisters'

I roar awake
my bum is cold
I shout
'TAKE COURAGE SISTERS –
BY THE THROAT AND STRANGLE IT!'

GIRL STALK

My blue stocking friend
we slobber together
like actresses –
we do not use tongues,
sharp as dainty shivs
we spit with
intonation.

MAGGIE HARRIS

MAGGIE HARRIS was born in New Amsterdam, Guyana, and
emigrated to England in 1971. An artist, she has exhibited
her paintings in Kent and at the Mall Galleries. Poetry has
been her main means of creative expression in recent years.
She has been published in *Poetry Now*, *First Time* and
Wasafiri. She received special mention by the South East
Arts Writers Group Prize 1991 for her poem 'Black Man on
Broadstairs Beach'. She is currently in her first year at
university doing Caribbean Studies.

'Further Education' was first published in Wasafiri
in 1991.

FURTHER EDUCATION

postcard drop through the door
                London bus circling Piccadilly
just here for a week   it read
so sorry schedule won't allow   a visit
well I went to mih bed and I cry for the friend that I lost
           to Further Education

we grow up with Ramsinghs, Narsinghs, Bonapartes
Foo-Young, Chu-Wong, Farquhartes
grandmother riding donkey cart
shaming the son in the concrete house
the lawyer daughter gliding round town
sad face hanging out Mercedes window
        glaze up safe up
        on the way up
        on the way to
           Further Education

but me and Ramawattie
liming round the town

hanging round street corners
paying for the lime
with a licking from the wild

                cane

      like we wild
for risking we reputation

why bother crying?   partner, comfort, mystified
  people grow apart   you can't expect
    things remain the same   schooldays can't come again

but I would never have cross that Atlantic
I woulda never swan round New York
without going for knock at Ramawattie door

letter drop through the door
        I ❤ N Y stamp bright
can't beat London for culture   it read
got to know my way around   so well
sorry schedule couldn't allow   a visit
been so busy since our return
imagine, they install the wrong colour jacuzzi!
I just don't know when these people will learn   and
Gopaul and I so involved with our thesis you know
you get nowhere, nowhere at all without   Further Education

FRANCESCA

Francesca bared her American bottom
white and unashamed
to our indrawn breaths of horror
at the Blairmont pool where estate cane
shared air with the Berbice River

in our culminated modesties
(Hindus and Catholic)
we extricated bathing suits

from beneath blue jeans and towels
like brassieres from under nighties
with dexterity

Francesca turned my mother's face pale
turning up on Christmas day
the bicycle ring and the 'Ma-a-rgaret!' cry
piercing the Sunday-quiet of our street
while flip-flops up front steps revealed
the don't care damn 'attitude' in tee shirt and shorts
       Francesca.
She awed me with her do's
while I strained under don'ts.

Francesca and I spent Saturdays
playing Smokey Robinson
drowning out the fish sellers
the Church bells
and Indira's mother downstairs yelling
to get her lazy head outa that book
and start the blasted cooking

We'd cycle over Canie Bridge in mini skirts and laughter
where Indian children turned to stare
and past rumshops where our daring easily
turned into fear

Francesca brought shame on my head
(and to her colour, they said)
our unisons against the world
were feeble against such structure

She disappeared like they all did
back to where she came from
melting into chrome and automobiles
where her quest for freedom blazed a trail
with blazing guns of sun browned legs and sounds
of Motown

leaving me the poorer
and the richer

THE WEAVER

Your story needs a thousand nights
or a Rumpelstiltskin
But it is only I, the fabric of your threads.

Your history is unfinished. Lost births on East Coast villages
unrecorded. Tales of a white father
smiling into sepia, black and white Sunday best.
Ancestorless, co-running plantations.

Mother, Portuguese. Also ancestorless. Only her womb
as host to you and her death through fear
on a jumbie backsteps, remembered. Dual purpose,
two seeds bored in the hole of the mind and left.

Sisters, two, locked away in a convent on the Georgetown coast
Mother-love replaced by staggered Auntie-visits
travelling across the Berbice River and fifty miles
by donkey cart   love warm on cold Rosary beads
pressed into trembling palms

You wove me stories in our senses land
where pictures grew in the imagination
unfettered by TV.   Of black James, your brother
rising from empty tar barrels in the night, for a joke
only his eyeballs glowing white from the ebony velvet
of skin and night;

You wove us stories to keep us occupied in the warmth
and smell of earth from the rain. Rainstorm, the Amerindian Eve
crying again. Trees heavy with coconuts drum – accompaniment
to your song. Protected in our wooden house on its sturdy legs
and the church at the bottom of the street.

Stories of your transplantation time up country and your other mother
rinsing evil out with holy water and if not, pointer broom.
Of your brother, his blonde hair shining on Corentyne streets
a-mingle with others transplanted from Delhi, Madras
and mother-seeds dug up from the deep bore holes of Africa.

His hair had fallen like straw, cauterized by typhoid
and whilst the room heaved with Catholic prayers, you
carrying buckets of water   amidst the incense and
the pointer brooms storing all into your consciousness
another sapling to grow.

Your story needs a thousand nights
or a Rumpelstiltskin
But it is only I, the fabric of your thread.

Stories, tales, in pieces that don't fit, that never repeat
the same another time; like life, tinting, picking up
from this mind and that mind.
But so what?

Your own identity fed to you like pieces of cake,
only what is sufficient. How much you know, censored.
Your youth, having no power had to be guided by others;
age seventeen into marriage. And only when my father died
did I too, learn more.

You climbed the years like steps, most times upward
with a step or two a-linger, a step or two a-back
your children weaving strength into the paradigm of Mother
your pride gathering force through the paradigm of Wife
your duty finding bond through the paradigm of God
and with re-transplantation in the name of immigration
you dug up your seeds from your deep bore holes
again.

Your story needs a thousand words
or a Rumpelstiltskin,
and I am but a pattern in the woven.

TAMAR HODES

TAMAR HODES was born in Israel in 1961 and educated in London and at Cambridge. She lives in North Staffordshire and teaches Creative Writing at Keele University. She also works freelance as a journalist for the BBC.

'Some Fly, Some Settle' won the R.D. Smith award for Young Poets in 1986.

ABIGAIL

Amid the lego
fallen like debris on a building site,
cups of tea and headless gingerbread men,
my friend and I talk (or try to)
punctuated by appeals –
'More juice, please,'
or 'Look what I've made.'
And my friend, distraught,
tells me about her daughter,
how she has disobeyed again.
'What this time?' I ask,
not really listening,
watching the children,
wishing I could play.

The previous night,
Abigail, the wicked daughter,
unlocked the door as they slept
and danced on the grass
in the bulleting rain.
'We've tried smacking
but it has no effect.'
And I look at Abigail,
four, sensual,

her face like an angel,
and I wish I could be her,
young, shiny, my bare feet
pressing on the spongy grass,
the rain making rivers down my cheeks,
my nightie twirling in the night.

I clutch my cup for comfort
and feel the hot tea burn my palms.

SOME FLY, SOME SETTLE

Flies his kite, the old man
on Parliament Hill.
Red bows. A string of freedom

The lily opens

I do not love you, she whispered
coffee burning the pot.

White

Paper on pavements.

Blown

Heron floods clouds.
The kite, the old man,
Parliament Hill.

Still

Skies close.
Men on dirty trains.
The drawing of blinds.

The lily closes

Kites fold.
Dead moths are brushed from window sills.

The lily locks

JEHANE MARKHAM

JEHANE MARKHAM was born in 1949 and studied painting.
She has had poems published in anthologies and has written
plays and features for the BBC. She lives with an actor and
has three sons.

HARD LINES

I dream of faces looking in,
Then I pass my baby up
through the broken windscreen.

We lie on the verge as if sunbathing;
A helicopter takes us to hospital
Like film stars in a glamorous rush.

I feel desperate like the White Queen,
But I smile at you,
Being processed under a black machine.

You are sent to SOINS INTENSIFS,
For the dangerously ill,
I and the boys have plenty of time to kill;

We sit on a bed eating caramel rice.
The nurses are chic but very nice,
'Viens, coco,' they say, as they wash the blood from the baby's face.

Tears gather in a hot secret way,
A choking necklace,
To be stored inside my throat for another day.

I search for you down the long, clean corridors.
In a blue moonless room you lie,
Under the caress of strange hands, unable to cry.

Red and white fluids curve in and out of you
Instead of wings.
You smell bad, of broken things.

As the words wont unfold,
You give me your familiar hand to hold.
Damp fingers on the sheet.

A nurse comes to show me out,
Her hair is beautifully combed in lines of gold,
She walks ahead without love heavy in her feet.

LIFE ON EARTH

Glistening violet grey
You lie folded down
Like a hot stone on the pillow.
A metallic fragrance is on your skin
I breathe you in
You smell of the darkness within.
The inner chambers where you grew
Soft bones hardening day by day
Wrapped in satiny membranes
And fed with strings of blood.

You have come through time
Bringing traces of early man
On your flattened face.
You remind me of things that grow under leaves
In the forest, dense organic matter
Fattening without light.

I was in a seacave
Feeling the suck and bite
Of pain arching out in the night.
I thought I was drowning
But I caught the tail of your comet in flight
And we fell to earth
Through a galaxy of eyes and hands
Into the golden light of the bedroom.

Hardly have the seconds ticked upon you
And you are transforming from stone to flesh
You grow exquisite in one breath.
The midwife weighs you in a tiny sling
Roses stand in the jug and sing.
Your ancient ancient eyes look calmly at the rest
Already we are putting your crab shaped arms
Into a white sleeved vest.

MARY McCANN

MARY McCANN lives in Edinburgh and belongs to
Pomegranate Women's Writing Group. She has had work
published in anthologies: *Sleeping with Monsters, The Crazy
Jig* (Polygon), *Fresh Oceans, Pomegranate* (Stramullion).

'Working for Moloch' was first published in the *Edinburgh
Women's Liberation Newsletter*, 'Blue Moon' in *Graffiti*;
'Packets of Light' in *Sempervivum;* and 'My Friend Marain
the Artist' in *Pomegranate* (Stramullion).

WORKING FOR MOLOCH

the cleaners are scrubbing the Institute lavatories
because women are supposed to do that

the girls are typing in the Institute offices
because women are dedicated and careful

the women are assembling printed circuits
because women are good at delicate work
and women's eyes are expendable

the young men are doing their PhDs
because young men are obedient and ambitious
and someone wants warheads
laser rangefinders
hunt and destroy capabilities
multichannel night seeking radar
and science is neutral

back home the wives of the PhD students are having babies
because women are maternal and loving
and who else can have children but women?

at the top of the tower the old men and the middle aged men
and sometimes one woman professor
meet to form plans, cadge funds and run the place
because obedient young men turn into obedient old men
and it's all for the good of the country
and defence funds are good for science
and science is neutral
and no one notices Moloch

the women bring them
clean toilets
cups of coffee
typescripts
micro circuits oh so neatly assembled
and children

and it's hard to see Moloch because he is both far away and
        everywhere
and they work on, priding themselves in their work
and no one asks to whom they are all obedient

and they say, 'Who's Moloch?   Never heard of him'
as out in the dark Moloch belches
and grows redder and redder
and fatter and fatter
as he eats the children

BLUE MOON

once
in a blue moon
you   took
a stroll past my window &
once
in a blue fit
I   cried
for the moon you carry in your pocket

and once moon
twice blue &
once bitten
I once in a blue song
sang for you
like a new shoe
and blew it all
I
in
you —
once moon
never forgotten

PACKETS OF LIGHT

child picks up
packets of light

amber and gold
and green, green
from the sea

child stores light
wraps it up
puts next to skin

child goes away
lives in dark houses

child becomes adult
slowly

packets of light
sit on shelf
behind clever books

times   pass

adult child's mother
becomes old, frightened

adult child goes back
back
back

visits old woman
in dull room

takes out packets of light
from pocket
lays on bedspread

breaks   seal

MY FRIEND MARAIN THE ARTIST

from a postcard of a painting by the same name by Mary McGowan

my friend Marain the artist
sits in a field full of flowers

she is fat and golden
black hearts scatter her dress

green irises bend their sharp leaves to her
blue black iris flowers whisper in her ear

her black eyes look out intently
as her pen scribbles on the board on her knee

casually, easily, as natural
as mending a sock, or nursing a baby

her hand moves, sketches, pauses
her eyes look and look

she plants her feet in the flowers
sits astride

knees apart, like a grandma
she doesn't care who sees her knickers

the red of the flowers has got into her hair
it coils and springs round her head

her breasts bounce with the sweep of her arm

my friend Marian the artist
drawing the world

CHRISTIAN McEWAN

CHRISTIAN McEWAN was born in London in 1956 and grew up in the Scottish Borders. She studied at Cambridge and Berkeley, and has held many jobs including gardener, teacher of creative writing, literacy adviser and construction worker. She has edited *Naming the Waves: Contemporary Lesbian Poetry* (Virago, 1988) and has poems widely published in magazines and anthologies, including *Granta* and *Sinister Wisdom*. She lives in New York.

GIRLS ETC

All year she was in love with cobalt blue,
An awkward passion, hard to satisfy.
She told me she loved girls – it wasn't true.

I loved her up and down and through and through.
I told her *woad*, a person has to try.
All year she was in love with cobalt blue.

I bought her something old and something new,
Borrowed a shirt the color of the sky,
Said I loved cobalt also (quite untrue).

I see it now, I said, the *primal hue* –
You have converted me. I cannot lie.
All year I've been in love with cobalt blue.

Astonishing! she said. I mean, you too!
Remove that shirt. It's time for us to fly.
She thought she loved me, but it wasn't true.

She loved that limpid and translucent blue,
Those royal dusks that make you want to cry.
She'd given up her heart to cobalt blue.

And really, there was nothing I could do.
I begged, I wept, I said that I would die.
I swore I loved her (not, by then, quite true).

I loved her love, as though she had the flu.
Some ache in her repeating, why, oh why,
Why girls when I'm in love with cobalt blue,
How could I love them? How could that be true?

IN THE TIGER CAGE

Each month it comes
the night I offer up to blood

The tiger roaring from inside the bars
the thin ache oozing down exhausted walls

Stinking meat in my belly-pit

Time now for some shadowy zoo-keeper
to open the doors

★

Another broken night
with a child up crying

and that child me

I sit on the stone pedestal
watching the hours

the door, the dust-balls,
the corner of the small cold room

★

What was mauled long ago
that rises up whining and flinching?

What lies wounded on the floor of the tiger-cage
and cannot, cannot sleep?

★

Someone without mother or grandmother
to bend over soothing

Someone on her own

★

Only the worn elder sister
in her ragged shift

only she comes –

her elbow bent
around her thin-spined books

carrying in one uncertain hand
a tepid cup of tea

(pale camomile)
like urine drained from that bed-wetting one

that frightened nine-year-old

★

How they crouch on the icy floor
over the stone pedestal

offering the rags of their throats to the tiger god

How they clasp each other
through the bloody bars

huddling together, comforting each other
with half-remembered lullabies

★

Outside the night recedes
steady and unaromatic

and there's no lover in the flesh
no friend to that wild body

Just this thing which keens and craves
devouring its own spirit to give sustenance

This is the roaring in the night
This is the tiger

The belly of blood is calling
It is roaring for the belly of another pressed against it

roaring to be loved, to be inhabited
roaring for its own unborn children

And it roars and it roars

THE DISCIPLES

Church was once a week on Sundays
but each day on the low, wheeled trolley,
the same libations poured from the massed bottles:
whiskey gleaming trout-bright over the stones,
the foreign vodka, cool and inevitable.
Here was no Savior holding out his arms,
offering us bread and sour French wine. Just
the regiment of Perrier, the cans of beer,
the heavy silver bucket of the ice.
No, you can't touch, can't touch – said the mother voice
as we reached for Lea and Perrins
in its authoritative parchment coat, the small

expensive bottles of tomato juice.
We ducked away, obedient, came back again,
hungry for the lemon and the fresh mint leaves,
the salty peanuts in their scarlet foil,
the corkscrew and the bottle-opener,
ridged and gleaming knives.
We were Catholics, they said. This was our altar.
Those shining upturned glasses were
the armies of our spirit. And
this was our Communion: the sour blue fizz
of Schweppes, the blocks of ice,
the thin sweet lime juice in the ordinary water
doing its clean dissolve.

LOIS McEWAN

LOIS McEWAN was born in 1962 in Edinburgh. She read
English at Aberdeen University before moving to London
to work as a journalist. She is now married and works on a
newspaper in North Queensland, Australia.

ZABRUSKA

Zabruska sits in the skeleton tree
Branches map her seaweed hair against the sky
Won't come down and she can't fly.

On a midnight swim down the river of love, she sings
I met my demon king
He ate my heart as I pulled him in
And drowned him deep,
Under my marble heart he sleeps.

ENDEAVOUR

Sailing past mangroves rooted in slime,
snakes coiled round stalks and scaly crocodiles.
Lord, give us shelter from the storm this night;
the compass needle quivers fit to break,
let not the wind our creaking timbers strike.

Magnetic boulders pull the arrow hard as gold,
black hawks circle burnt pink cliffs
under livid cloud lit from below,
velvet bats flap leather wings in purple dusk,
palm fronds sweep the sand.

Black men underneath the trees,
butterflies smeared on their eyes;
death creeps from my savage heart,
first ashore my pistol fires.

INSOMNIA

I woke to feel the air stir on my face
and see the comets burn across the sky.
Over the waves stars fell into the sea
As night falls toward orange morning, sun to see

OBITUARY

After Coronation Street we light the fire
and sit. Nana knits up
vests to send to Africa,
fingers clicking to and fro,
while I unwound the rotten wool
and coiled it on the coals:
it bubbled for a second with her spit
and clung like veins to bone.

BLISS

Unborn soul signalling,
bird on a wire,
let me draw you into my second skin,
swim through evolution in the womb
come soon: be born complete

KATHLEEN MCMULLEN

KATHLEEN MARY McMULLEN was born in County Cork,
Ireland in 1960 and educated in England, Italy and
Botswana. She worked for the women's movement in the
1980s and is now active in the Campaign Against the
Arms Trade.

THE VALLEY OF GIANT LOCUSTS

Come my friend
and let me take
you to a land
so strange
your tender dreams
will cry aloud in grief –

Come and see
the swollen earth –
the empty space –
ancient folds of time
creeping over
naked lime and slate –

Come and see
the darkening sun –
the ruby globe –
ash/smoke –
the trembling
end of dawnlight day –

Look – there!
Beyond the frozen
peaks – Do you see
the land of rising
dust? The valley
of giant locusts?

Watch them eat
with jaws larger
than God's bulldozers!

Watch them eat
and eat and eat –

slender grass –
fragrant weed –
timeless seed –

Their purpose
is not to wonder why
Their purpose
is to feed and die –

LIFFEY TURNIP THE FARMER'S DAUGHTER
LUSTS AFTER THE SON OF AN ENGLISH QUEEN

Once I desired you –
Once I lusted after
                      you –

Tongue, lips
Fingers, saddle . . .

You have all of these
Enough to keep me
                      happy –

Chorus:
For he's a jolly good
                    fella
For he's a jolly good
                    fella!

Liffey:
Then the day arrived
When I realised

I'd never get to bed
The protestant son

Of an English
Queen –

An Irish lass I be
An Irish lass, sì, sì!

Chorus:
For she's a jolly good
                    welder
For she's a jolly good
                    welder
For she's a jolly good
                    welder
AND SO SAY ALL OF US!

TYRANNY RECYCLED

England, you done
            me wrong –
From the gutter
            to the ghetto
From the ghetto
            to the gutter
You done me wrong –

Like a scientist
     dressed in silk
You kept me at
     an objective
Distance –

You divided me –
     examined me –
Imprisoned me –
     savaged me –

From the gutter
     to the ghetto
From the ghetto
     to the gutter
England, you done
     me wrong
All along –

MADELINE MUNRO

MADELINE MUNRO has been published in *Ambit* and *Stand*
and won prizes in national competitions. She grew up on a
Highland farm and has taught in schools in the south-east
of England.

THE CHANT

Say, 'Frock, frock; Janet, Janet.'
Her mother's plan, the chant,
to put away the morning's dread
along the two mile road to school;
hold down the fear at night
past empty Tomashogle,
bare on the upper field,
unlit, and harbouring fright
before the darker edge of trees.
'Frock, frock; Janet, Janet.'
Round to the turn, the bend,
and then clear sight of home.

Tuesday, the market day
at Inverness. He had been
asked. Tonight her father
would bring home, under his arm,
the frock, maybe a box with something
more, and want his slippers
while it was unwrapped.
Now there was Janet, safe
in the byre, soft black
of the Jersey round the eyes –
and she could lead her like
a dog, for summer holidays
rope-haltered to Newmill.

'Frock, frock; Janet, Janet.'

What can we chant now to lift the dark?

BREASTS

The word was less difficult for her now,
perhaps. Of course, they always spoke

of chicken breast or breast of lamb
unthinkingly – even, too, breast stroke.

It was on the human mammary gland
that, somehow, the voice broke.

At school she had envied girls
who grew with small, neat breasts.

went running free. And she
was already past her best

before she knew what burdened her
was beautiful, what the upbeat west

desired and bought, the womanly –
as here in this documentary

where breasts were shaped and filled,
exposed in cosmetic surgery

to hands inserting implants
in a skilled upholstery.

Yet the craftsmanship could disappoint,
not last – like furniture

puffed out with some cheap
cushioning. And sad to endure

all this then dread a cancer
that was past a cure.

Still, television brings on
sadder scenes – tall women,

baring lifeless breasts,
who cling to the stricken

in the cropless sand. Or warlord
pilots – with their surgeon

tricks, target precision
from a high-tech sky –

who add now to their mission tally
mothers, their milk gone dry,

waiting in ill-lit hospitals
where the starved and festering die.

GIRL WITH RATS

I

Growing chilled
in the sunless precinct
we roll up our posters
of pathetic naked hens
and walk with the folded trestle
to her flat for tea.

The talk moves on to festivals
her singing; ley lines,
dowsing and healing;
the psychic or not.
Auras, she feels,
perhaps anyone can see.

Before we leave
we want to meet her pets.
She lets them perch
one on each shoulder –
a collar
of moving rats.

I stare
at the long-nosed faces
the bare, segmented tails,
try to distinguish
which one is timid
which one bold.

She lifts her arms
to rearrange them
carefully
holds them
beneath
the intellectual face.

II

It was through a window
late one night
a random prowler
picked her out.
She was lucky.
He left her there alive.

I first imagined
how he stopped and fled,
disturbed by the watching eyes,
let all the old
revulsions rise:
dark shapes

that bolt in shadow
through a wall;
vermin
they lunged at
yelling with pitchforks. –
on a threshing day.

But he had turned away
unhurriedly
(she lying
nose broken on some furniture
hands loosened
from her back)

and, taking time
for one last act,
he brought the smaller rat,
laid it
like flowers
upon her heart.

CAROLINE NATZLER

CAROLINE NATZLER's collection of short stories, *Water Wings* (Onlywomen Press), was published in 1990. She teaches writing at Goldsmiths College and the City University as well as working as a solicitor.

'I'M TALLER THAN YOU'

'I'm taller than you,' you'd laugh
Standing on my feet.

The best, the only.
The waste of the years before you.

We could talk about everything
The whole world in our embrace
Hugging closer and closer until
There was not much world left.

Then you stood on my feet
And flew.

And now? Beyond this wide ache
The world, perhaps.

With only something missing
And I not grounded,
Loose.

'I SLIP AROUND'

I slip around, slight inside
My grandmother's great tweed coat.
Did she walk so tall?
Have I yet, at forty, the authority
To wear it?
Broad on my shoulders as borrowed armour
Grave as a heavy hand on my shifting life.

London taxis roll by
Bowler hat black, splashes of orange lamplight
Sliding deceitful over the roofs. None empty.
Smug in each, men and women riding forward.

Behind, the park drips in the dusk.
On the edge of the pavement
I forget where I'm going.

And rustling in the low pocket, a shred of paper.
My fingers brush it, like moths.

A space, indifferent, cool
Between me and the silk soft lining.
This coat hangs straight
Sturdy as the walls of an empty castle.

My grandmother, Head of the family
The sort of woman of whom stories are told
Dominant, tricky, humorous
A woman with servants and a sharp tongue.
She taught my mother tennis and never knew how to cook
Left all her money to her sons, though she loved my mother best
Walked in this coat in thick stockings and firm shoes
Knowing what she was about.

Not I,
Streaks of love, dissolved, misty now
Some shafts of pain
Indifferent jobs, some poems brooding tight in a drawer
And hollow evenings watching TV news
Thinking, politics is for people with families
Urgent for their childrens' future.
Not I
Pausing on the kerb.

Crinkling a piece of paper, knuckle-moulded
Mine perhaps, though I've forgotten.
A friend's note – an idea scrawled –
A womens' protest leaflet . . .

Smooth as a sleeping cat
The space between me and this coat.
It has no shape but its own
Heavy hang

YOUR HOME, OCTOBER 27TH

It's fitting, like the shadow drag of pain,
I'm here the day the clocks go back.
After the sheltering years
when I fed you with the wide world's emptiness
to hold you fast,
after the raw years alone,
I'm here the day the clocks go back.

You are not feeling well.
Your new lover (too mild this one
with her almond eyes for me to curse)
is away
playing her violin in a distant city, and calm.
Today the clocks go back.

Fragile on the sofa you shift,
make a quiet joke, pleasing yourself;
a quick lipped smile to the corner
as if I were not here,
as if you could shrug off
the mist of winter greying the windows.
Today the clocks go back.

We drink a little, turn to the TV's slick vitality
and when you click your glass down
and the ice rattles
I think it's someone tapping at the window pane.

TODAY

In a way the miracle is happening.
(But in its own way, let it take its course)
One cannot go back, I know,
But today,
After the jagged, dark time
Riven
– You wrenched my life from me, leaving –
Today, we walked in the park again
And you remembered our old blarney about the ducks
Good, sweet, morally pure, you used to say,
Boring, ugly, morally indifferent, I . . .
And you remembered the first poem you wrote for me.
And said you'd dreamed recently of my garden
Squelching, clogged with clinging frogs, some dead, you'd sown
As a few casual seeds. You felt guilty
Sorry.

And in the park today, I think,
We both remembered the two fingernail frogs
Like tiny brown hearts, bounding
Leaping from our feet on the first walk.
'Such optimism,' you'd said then, and held my hand.

After the screaming time, flung out in the dark to die
Suspended in pain,
In the park today, I wanted to say
Not your fault, not all your fault
The multiplying and cloying;
Three piece suites and heating bills
Dependency, tears, competition
Grey Sunday walks in the park
Bound in duty like our parents
Boredom and jealousy. And some dying.
Not just your fault.

After the dark strangled time
Tightening myself to solitude
Finding myself again (morally pure, at least,
The wronged woman, thought I) while you leapt off
To passion, the free spirit and the lesbian turmoil
(Morally irresponsible, thought I)
In the park today
You remembered for us
Our beginning.

After the gut pull of knowing
The ache and the wailing were old
In me before, not just you;
And after the time away, watching sunlight cut
And flow on foreign rivers, and cold mornings light
Each day new to the place and growing real
And the little words coming like winter birds,
Let go – nothing to lose – release;
In the park today, I thought
Time has flowed.

After the first brittle meetings
To test this notion, friendship
Arch, proclaiming politics, gossip, jobs, the validity
Of our separate cut-glass lives,
In the park today
We talked
And hugged, before parting.

And though I cried a little in the rattling train
Back to my house, empty but stalwart now
And though I didn't say this to you
And perhaps will not,
In the park today I thought
This is it. The miracle is happening
But in its own way, let it take its course.
Perhaps
After all, we can move beyond our end
As well as our beginning.

BUNMI OGUNSIJI

BUNMI OGUNSIJI is the first daughter of Yoruba parents. She says, 'I am passionately committed (and indebted) to those who reflect me. I discover myself daily in the faces, the life experiences of my people, I write to remember, to give back, to mourn, to celebrate, to fly.'

FLIP-FLOPS & WRAPPERS: TOKENS OF LOVE

i don't think you saw me laughing
in daddy's oversized flip-flops
back-flaps smacking at my tiny soles
and me cat-walking on your
bedroom rug,
me twirling, twirling in your
sun-splashed wrapper and getting dizzy
on my grown up gear . . .
and i've never told you how,
when the world seemed to be laughing at me
in my navy blue bell-bottoms
which hung like wings around my ankles
how when they stuck out raspberry jelly
tongues at me,
made ice-cream faces at the xmas party,
made me feel like minnie mouse
in moonboots
because i had my hair in bunches
too many feet high
and my heels in silver platforms
too many inches off the ground,
how
i felt safer in those things
when the whole world seemed
to be pointing at me

laughing at me
there i stood
a dimpled stick-insect
feet lost in oversized flip-flops
twig-thighs draped in patterned wrappers
acting some big woman
and laughing laughing right back
and loving you then
i forgot that it was you
who had given me
the bell-bottoms
to wear.

CHRISTMAS EVE

i remember the small blue dining-room
cluttered with bags
of gari and stock-fish
and the limping lady
with the criss-cross eyes
who came to buy them . . .

and with me now you move
in your seasonal evening concoction
mixing aromas to ooze
from momoyin sealed tight
in crackling foil
and peppered jolof rice
mushy, red
delicious and hot,

and i'd like to learn to cook
akra a crisp golden brown
to fry plantain so it tastes
moist to the last bite,

to make okra stew gooey

and melting in a thousand
green and white pieces
on my tongue

i can just about see you
working a kind of magic
in your eight oclock kitchen
all misty to the windows
and crammed ceiling high
with scrumptious smells of sorts . . .

and i can barely touch
in my mind's eye
the fraying outline of your wrapper
sadly dim in black and white
as the shade is cut unclear,
but your hands

are vivid
and fast, so fast
moulinexing bean powder
dicing boiled liver
chopping onion
salting puree
slicing egg . . .

and i remember your little
market-from-home
and the odd shaped yams you sold

i'd like one day
to move contentedly amidst
my own yuletide potions
and maybe have
a
daughter
watching
me.

A POEM FOR ESSEX

to quote a dumb cliché
you don't know me
but i know you . . .

see
last night
you smacked me square upside my head
socked me with a glove of piercing hard-talk
then fanned me with a glowing rushing
sensitivity

you had me
buzzing and spinning
and crazy on literature
sucked me whole into your whirlwind
of sheer sincerity
and let me up sometimes for air . . .

you took me
from spectator's seat to intimate corner
and guided me down your river
of calm of anger
of fear of love

you opened out
to let me fall head first
into a tumbling score of night music
so refreshing in its newness
it completely overwhelmed . . .

you were
spitfire
pouring lava
imposing questions

you were
a balmy stream
massaging earlobes
caressing minds . . .

you did
something with words
that should be certified a sin
you shook them up inside and out
got them living walking personified
had them probing into private souls
had them hynotise revitalise
made them treacle-hot
and stirring innards into motion

you had them
flowing plaintively
tugging heart strings
drawing tears . . .

you had them
playing comical
curling mouths
and busting ribs . . .

you swept me
off my feet
spun me a line
to whip me
out of
apathy

you knocked me into knowing
eased me into feeling
held me on the crest of a magical wave

you hooked
me round your poet's finger
hauled me in
enthralled me
spoke to me
gave to me
shared with me

so now
to coin a new cliché
you don't know me
but for that black and wonderful hour
i was
you.

LINDA ROSE PARKES

LINDA ROSE PARKES was born in Jersey. She has two
children and teaches in adult education in Aachen,
Germany. She has been published in a wide range of
magazines including *The Rialto, Writing Women, Orbis, Wide
Skirt, Outposts, Wayfarers* and *Envoi*. Her work appears in
the Women's Press anthology, *In the Gold of the Flesh*, 1990.

JEFFREY'S LEAP★

i

You say you wore brocade for him?

> I thought I was safe   son of my
> father's friend   family knowing family

You say you wanted that first kiss?

> I tried to pull away

Would you not say you led him on?

> didn't mean him to go so far   I thought
> I was safe   after that first kiss I
> tried to pull away

Did you not desire him?

> I don't know what he heard   my voice
> buckling under him

Have you not had other men?

> his dead weight panicking me

★ Jeffrey's Leap, a rock so named in Jersey C.I. after the legend of Jeffrey,
sentenced to death for rape by leaping from this rock. Surviving the first
jump, he jumps again.

Could one not indeed say   that you
are responsible?

>   I don't know what he heard
>   the stone shards breaking through my skin
>   ripping the brocade   my voice buckling

Would you not say that you
are responsible?

>   It wasn't me who told on him   I knew
>   what they would do   the rumours
>   my father's shame

ii

Son of her father's friend
Family knowing family
Of good standing in the community.

>   I had to get out   would have taken her
>   with me   burn through her soft walls
>   to another womb   another heritage

Were you not the oldest son
First in line
For your father's wealth?

>   I pitted myself when she fought   felt myself
>   flicker   about to go out   I had to burn
>   through her

Would you not say she led you on?
After that first kiss   did she try
To pull away?

>   I had to get out
>   to the gulls ricocheting off the water
>   I wanted to take her with me   I had to get out
>   I pitted myself

iii

Did you jump   or did the halberdiers push
From the sin and death symmetry of this black rock?

> I closed my eyes   prayed only for the
> soothe   and final
> I remember my vertigo of fear
> how the sea loomed up out of the sky

The held breaths   the drum roll
Ocean blinding with foam

Women gathering   heightening their
Lives with handsome   carnal eventfulness.

Did you try for the fluke in the rocks?

> There were no women   I simply closed
> my eyes   the women were kept at home
> that day

But the tide was high   kept you
From the rocks this time   swimming
Back safely
– Women hitching up their skirts
To clamber down to you

> There were no women
> I did not choose to leap again
> longed only to lie down   blank as the sky
> blown across by clouds

Now egged on by vanity
Thinking to enter the pardon
Of God's womb   which you had seen
The first time down as shoals of golden fishes
Manning the waterways and gulleys
– Each one a woman soul –   you
Leaped a second time

> I did not choose to leap again

You say it was the soldiers?
Hating loose ends   seeing quirk
In their design   insisting   You Geoffroi
Plumb God again   leave nothing to Chance?

        I did not choose to leap a second time

iv
You say you wore brocade for him?
Would you not say you led him on?
That you desired him?
Indeed you wanted that first kiss
And have you not had other men?
And could one not say
That you are responsible
For his breaking his head
Among the bladderwrack and gulls?

        It wasn't me who told on him   I knew
        what they would do   the rumours   my father's
        shame   I tried to pull away   my voice buckling
        under him   I don't know what he heard
        his dead weight panicking me   entering my heart

v
Your screams in the far-off waterlight of stars
    break on another Isle.

Now only the rock remains

MAKING LOVE TO POSEIDON

    Kittiwakes preen in his keel;
    half in sleep he couples the sky, breeze,
    sun falling all over him.

    What longing slams through my clothes
    to steal his salt?

Crouching in his shallows
fingering his blue-green colluding surfaces,
the sun warms my buttocks
the wet sand I dig my heels in.

Cupping his surly, power-hungry spume
into my lap
I no longer dream of wedding robes
– he has never been less quarrelsome,
more close –

        with me taking
        what he gives unknowingly:

        his sea anemones
        his salt-sea fishes
        swimming in me now.

DISCOVERY POEM

They filter through somehow
the old taboos
though my mother never said
'it's dirty' or 'you'll go blind'.

But my daughter can't sleep
buries her head in the pillow, cries.
Eleven p.m.
It's too bad to tell.

With hugs I ease it into the light.
Assure her it's natural
that I was the same
did the same things.

I am forty, she is nine.
I don't say how long it took
for me to love myself.

She clings to me, I stroke her arm.
She has pubic hair, breasts like baby voles.
Hovers at mirrors, uses passion fruit on her skin.
Wants to be sylph-like, princessy –
not tall, strong; with this need between her thighs.

Again I tell her she is beautiful.
She smells of soil, gorse and peat.
Of a bird flown over fields:
she smells of the warm
in the crook of its wings.

CATE PARISH

CATE PARISH was born in the USA and lives and works in
Britain as a primary school teacher. She has had poems
published in *The Rialto, Other Poetry, Staple, Resurgence* and
several other magazines. She has also had work included in
In The Gold of the Flesh (Women's Press, 1990).

MEDUSA

On the South bank, with Big Ben as the backdrop,
a model is flouncing back and forth along a 3-foot line.
To convey the requisite gay abandon
she swings her hair and handbag at exact intervals

like an obsessive executing rituals.
Her smiles and pouts alternate like traffic signals.
The cameraman knows what he wants,
and he isn't getting it. It's the hair –

it doesn't toss up uniformly, but coils out all over.
He stops shooting at intervals to flatten it
with a professional hand that imitates stroking.
They'll have to keep an eye on her conditioning.

Some little girls with jumpropes swing
blindly into the scene. He thumbs them out.
Just outside the frame hover the short, fat,
unexhibitable women with even bloodier hair

whose eyes are hard as stones. Later they'll buy the image
spred flat with open mouth and hair tossed back,
swinging its handbag over the golden clock.
As if it's a she who's on top of the world.

THREE WOMEN

Herself, her mother, and her grandmother
set separately around the room
like un-nested Russian dolls.
Somehow the smallest one
had once contained the bigger two.
The biggest one, herself, still feels the smallest
and obliges them by knitting on for hours
to prove she uses what they taught her.

They fill the time by watching her.
She senses voids inside them
but can't now provide fulfilment
(just this spurious knitting of space)
while inside herself she feels
not the incipience of yet another Russian doll

but the surprise reward
for the one who arrives at the end of the series
a tiny solid gold statuette
standing all on its own.

PASCALE PETIT

PASCALE PETIT was born in Paris. She has an MA in
sculpture from the Royal College of Art, and has exhibited
widely. She works as an artist-in-schools on GAIA projects,
and is co-editor of *Poetry London Newsletter*. Her poems have
been published in *London Review of Books*, *Poetry Review*,
The North, *Poetry Wales*, *The Rialto*, *Poetry London Newsletter*,
and in several anthologies.

'Ice-fall Climbing in Tibet' has been published in *The
North*.

ICEFALL-CLIMBING IN TIBET

I am facing the icefall at the base of Everest.
A great white city is slowly subsiding.
The walls are never the same, never quiet.
An avalanche lands with a suppressed sigh.
I put on my crampons, sharpen my axe,
pass through the gate, which collapses after me.
Some of the rooms have crumbled. Some are lit
by the blue and pink lamps of my mother's house.
I wipe the window which reveals our lounge.
Mother is rocking. Her rhythm drives the city
over the cliff. Her rhythm keeps her warm.
She is knitting me a cardigan white as snow.
Her eyes are the windows of a deserted home.
I tap on the ice, but she can't see. I want
to ask her why she settled here, her dream
of travelling to Tibet, to religious air.
Her chair begins to melt, and I am scratching
at ice packed in annual layers which recede
to the beginning of time. A wall topples,
but I have arrived, and I will go on,
digging my spikes into a vertical façade

until I reach a bedroom window, the master-bed
with no master, the mistress of the house, ill.

There is a blue lampshade on the bedside table,
and a dressing-table with the towers and domes
of my mother's make-up, perfumes, jewellery-box.
A powder-puff lies abandoned, the powder spilt.
My mother's face is blue. She is lying under the quilt
which she made, sewing the patches of her life
into a stained-glass mosaic, over the church of her body.
I am bending over her with a cup of tea, a bunch of flowers,
a loveletter, breakfast. She wakes. She eats. She
gets better. She moves house. I want to carry her away,
but the city is groaning. Crowds swarm the streets
then are buried alive. Other windows are atriums.
In them are forests. There are riots. Cars are smashed.
An axe breaks the plate-glass and trees wither.
The city is shaking under the stampede of my family.
Parts form meltwaters. A bridge sinks into a river.
I recognise Paris, London. I have lived in both.
I see myself as a child playing under the Eiffel Tower,
then as an adult, living near Alexandra Palace
the day it caught fire. The exits have caved in.
There is nothing I can do but take a room and live here.

ICEFALL-CLIMBING IN TIBET II

Every adventurer has heard of the great white city
which is the gateway to Everest. It is fed
by the Khumbu Glacier, only to collapse over
a cliff, in a series of seracs the size of hotels.
The city wants citizens. There are rooms to let.
When the sun shines, cracks gape in the pavement,
claim the most seasoned climber. I must concentrate.

My crampon spikes must match the rungs of the ladder
propped over a crevasse. I am enclosed in the womb
of my headlamp, climbing by night, when the temperature
isn't so high that the ice thaws, isn't so low
that it snows. One snowflake is nothing in itself,
a cold word softly slipped in conversation. Larger flakes
sting the cheek. A snowstorm caused the avalanche
which buried my friend. I try not to think of his
deepfrozen body, embedded above previous corpses.
I am alert to the tremors of distant icequakes,
their effect on houses precariously balanced.

Like all capitals which are constantly rebuilt
with haphazard streets, there is an old quarter.
In the centre of the icefall, the buildings are blue.
Time is measured in annual bands. Rooms are packed
with records of past generations. The ice preserves
each birth, each orgasm, each death. The ice
groans so much I think I'm in a hospital. Everyone
is wearing white. There are wards of white faces
on white pillows, between crisp white sheets.
The operating-theatres are hung with icicles
of assorted pains, waiting for the patient to awake.

My friend has died. The sherpas are disheartened.
They chant mantras and won't carry my load.
They are removing the aluminium ladders. They
are packing. They burn incense to Chomolungma
– Goddess Mother Of The Land, whom I call Everest.
But I have seen the view from the Khumbu Glacier.
The white city is scaled. Already I am halfway up
the sky. The cautious ones, back at Base Camp,
seeing my headlamp, mistake me for a star.
I have to wear an oxygen mask, fight the sensation
that I have acquired a friend who eats half of my rations,
creeps into my tent, to make love to me nightly.

ANDROULA SAVVAS PISTOLAS

ANDROULA SAVVAS PISTOLAS was born in Birmingham of Greek-Cypriot and Irish parents. She is studying for a Master's Degree in Social Work at London University.

HAIRY RITA

Whore whore whore
she calls out
and they dig their nails into their
bellies and want to die.

Boss woman kicks,
(her nipples harden)
and they fall,
incongruous fall of milk heavy
women,
the dishes not washed,
the hum of talk-talk-talk drifts
through to the hall as she enters,
red rag bull goes mad
and kick (hard nipples)

Pitch black moon clear
and the door locked to save
her from the wolves,
Hairy Rita mashes her magic button and
her self dissolves
into starched white sheets.
She sees pictures in her head and
her eyes run fast into her ears,

Aahh, my boy my boy

and turns her back on the moon,
clenching her fist for another
day,
and her thighs fizz.

MAUREEN IS A FUNNY GIRL

But not so funny that people laugh.
She twists her face and stares at little boys,

They're mine they're mine

her rising lip her rising hand
and then the child is pulled away
and Maureen staring after,
tight fingers,
white marks on her palms.

Jesus loves me
wants me to look fine
oh yeah

and her skinny breasts
flip and slap
as she dances
encircling her nipples with red lipstick
and patting her freshly emptied belly,

ooohh baby baby

checking that other-woman-wife hasn't
dripped out of the wardrobe
then Jesus comes into the room and says
dance for me Maureen,
checks the wardrobe
and settles back to watch the show.

GRANDFATHER HOOK

Grandfather Hook lives and dies with a wolf
slung over his stooping back and
limp slide, sound his footsteps in the darkness
of my wallpaper.
Grandfather Hook has deformed feet, twisted toes
are writhing worms with yellow bellies. When I
hear his slow shuffle from looming corridors, greedy
worms wriggle on my back, biting small clean lumps along
the line of my spine, and never will I swim with this
sturdy cloak upon me, wrapped close like a shaky hand
across my mouth.
'Come, I can make paper moons to rise in the fire,
come, I will show you.'
So secret moons rose in the hair draped sky and the next
day, (the sun was smirking), the warm drip between my thighs
was blood and I thought I was dying, ebbing slowly into
white pants, while Grandfather's wolf howled between his
sobs.
In its bag the wolf would kick and I could see it struggling
for a birth into the world of men.
Other times Grandfather would gently free the wolf and it
would sit panting on the end of my bed, pricked with rosethorns,
tears in its yellow eyes.

WENDY RUTHROFF

WENDY RUTHROFF was born in 1930 and lived in a South
Yorkshire mining village until she went to university. It was
not until she was in her forties, training as a psychotherapist,
that she started to write. The first draft of 'Snow
Impressions' dates from this time.

SNOW IMPRESSIONS

Lie no more on me.
Your impression is
Like bird tracks in the snow,
Clean and clear,
Showing you were here
In the falling of the snow.
I have to go
I have to make the journey,
Back in the melting snow.

TO FISHER, ALMOST BLIND AT EIGHT

Fisher with pebble lenses, big eyed
You peer at books two inches from your nose.
Words like little fish dart and dash
In formations wild before you enclose
Them in the aquarium of the mind.
One day you lose your specs, so now
Can only sit, tiny eyed, as you swim
And surf the breakers of your mind.

GETTING READY FOR CHURCH

Respectability kisses me rigid
As I struggle to pour
The exhuberant flesh
Into the spandex mold.
Like a too stiff blancmange
I will not wobble.

Maureen Sangster

MAUREEN SANGSTER was born in Aberdeen and now lives in
Kirkcaldy, Fife where she works part-time as a tutor for the
Workers' Educational Association. Her poetry has been
published in various magazines and anthologies.

VICTORIAN FEMALE SERVANT

I who am
Come to this great house,
I who am
Lifted to this great house,
Worn down by poverty,
Keen with gratefulness,
I who am –
Thank you, sir, ma'am.

I who am
To share of a very neat room,
Window overlooks
Such a garden and
I who am
With others, watch the others.
I who am –
Thank you, sir, ma'am.

In the steaming kitchen
The boiled birds' beaks hiss
In your pies.
I who am
Serve as best I can, lay
The ballroom bright and grand,
Your glove, sir,
Thank you, sir – no, ma'am.

I who am
Shriek from the roof
'They are bats
These men in frock coats!'
Moving motionless,
Heavy homelessness,
My child – his
Underbellies this.

I who am
Less pretty not neat,
I who am
Hooked, my method
Metal knows
Birth as brief as death.
I who was,
Am, sir!

MUSEUMS

Museums
are keen on

eyes peering at
white labels
with minute black print on them

and eyes peering at
a truncheon, a patterned plate,
a black case, a brown leather wallet,
an open-barrelled gun, unloaded,
beside it 2 shiny bullets, a book,
another book, another wallet
all in one glass coffin
                with the lid on it.

Sometimes
emotion is at hand –
a tragic love affair
spins in a spiral
out, beyond the glass
and the fine letters
            of grief become our vocabulary

But usually categories of
            era
            make
            material
            theme
            apply

Never, never
have
all the blue, blue
            objects of the past
swept like a sea
into one museum room.

THROUGH THE LOOKING GLASS

through the looking
glass: your breasts
aren't flat,
their nipples startle.
after a drunken night
out we find ourselves
in bed together. When
will your boy-friend intrude?
When will mine? of course
we have
gone
through the looking glass
down

the
rabbit
hole into the Time Machine
forwards backwards
women
dream of this
it always is yet
Tomorrow
we'll begin again
our false liaison
with The World. Muddled by
the brrrrr
the whirr
our hoarse voices
will grasp the safe re-
lief of sameness
and in the office break
neither you nor I
shall mention us
but, desperately, through
our coats
our scarves
our rings
our skirts
our shoes
our hair
our colours
our breasts
we'll advertise
a man has you, a man has me
oh my love, our lie!

JAN SELLERS

JAN SELLERS is a part-time adult education worker, full-time lesbian and intermittent performance poet. Her poems have appeared in a range of magazines and anthologies.

'Waiting' was published in *Common Lives/Lesbian Lives* (USA, 1991); 'Where Lesbians Come From' in *Whatever You Desire* (Oscars Press, 1990); 'The Wolf' in *Poetry Matters* (Peterloo Poets, 1992).

BECOMING FOREST*

A place of hidden voices: many, one,
wind, water, willow, oak and filtered light.
Deep roots split rock and wrap their secrets tight.
Trees speak in tongues, in clustered clearings, strung
like beads of hollowed wood along a slope,
where unacknowledged moments, shadow-free
catch light in fragments: bird wings, bright through leaves,
clear of the ground and shadows shifting shape.

Time passes. Darkness circles. Trees can move
as seasons do; and roots can touch, birds nest,
old branches break, moss cover open ground.
Wind, water, night and daylight interweave
of many elements, a meeting place,
grown into harmony. A balance found.

* This poem is a reflection on living with Multiple Personality Disorder: learning to live both as one person and as many. It is dedicated to the friend who talked with me about her experiences.

WAITING*

Waiting in the dark
for the fire
waiting in the dark

I will become air.
Slide between bars.
Fly far and free –
where they cannot reach me,
oh my dear.

Hearing you burn last night
I felt you dying.
How can they touch me, now?
Your soul's a star,
shining through bars at me,
calling.
You've flown far,

leapt from the raging fire
they keep for me.
Leaping, a star in air,
a shining point,
a breathing space from fear.
Wait for me, beloved.
I'll join you there.

* In medieval times, women accused of lesbianism were sometimes burned at the
stake.

WHERE LESBIANS COME FROM

It is true that lesbians do not have families;
we have pretend family relationships.
We do not have mothers, fathers, brothers, sisters;
our sons and daughters do not count at all,
having no families within which to rear them.
And our lovers – there's nothing in that
but something mocking truth;
for you know it's true
that lesbians do not have families, like you . . .

We emerge, instead, complete from some dark shell,
beds and beds of us (like oysters,
what else would I mean?)
sea-born on stormy nights
with the wind in a certain quarter.
We rise and wriggle, all slippery and secret,
curling and stretching and glad to be alive,
untangling our hair from the wind and salt and seaweed.
We steal clothes from washing-lines,
and once it's daylight, almost pass for human.

Glowing into warmth in the sun or a hard north wind
we lick the salt from our lips,
for now. And smile.
We live for a while, in the light,
despite your brutal laws
and your wish that we were not here;
we return to our beds by moonlight
to nurture and foster the sweet salt shells
that give birth to our lesbian futures.
And there we plot, in our dark sea beds,
the seduction of your daughters.

THE WOLF

I cried wolf in the pasture. No-one came.
'This is the child,' they said, "who lied before,
who dreamt a wolf was scratching at her door,
and roused the town!" And so I took the blame.
I cried wolf in the night; they mocked my claim,
beat me and left me on the hard dirt floor
where I wept, cold and heartsick, bruised and sore,
knowing the beast they feared would come again.

My mind drifts out. A shadow on the moon,
a hunter in the night behind the storm,
I wait for the dark ending of the year.
See now, the window's open, and the tune
the wind plays, raises hackles. I change form.
I am the wolf child. It is I they fear.

CHERRY SMYTH

CHERRY SMYTH is Irish and lives in London. Her poetry is featured in various anthologies, including *Frankenstein's Daughter* (Stride Publications, 1993). She published *Queer Notions* (Scarlet Press, 1992).

'Maybe It Was 1970' was published in *The Popular Front of Contemporary Poetry* (Angel Press, 1992).

MAYBE IT WAS 1970

Kids my age play real soldiers,
dashing milk bottles bombs against tanks,
binlids for shields.
'That gun's as big as thon wee skitter.'
Mummy turns up the sound.
I'm missing Crossroads, leave the room loudly
and slip behind the kitchen curtain
to search for Derry burning.
The news is too far away.

Maybe it was 1970.
Bernadette Devlin shouting.
She was a student and
she was a MP.
She was a cheeky wee monkey.

On the news Dad's shop burning down.
My mascara had run.

Maybe it was 1973.
The reverend Ian Paisley
crushed through a window
on the telly.
His hand bled.

'For God's sake, this is madness. Go home.'
How could a minister be bad?
Blood ran freely down his wrist
like roads,
like the red hand of Ulster
    severed.

I was fifteen.
Miss Duffin announced in assembly,
'If this doesn't stop very soon,
it's double maths on Friday afternoon.'
The bombscares stopped.

Maybe it was 1977.
On the news Dad's shop burning down.
I was at Kelly's.
It came on in the bar.
I was in love with Shawn Logan.
I didn't know whether to kiss or cry.
I wanted him.   I wanted to go home.
He was much older.
He was a Catholic.
He held me in his car.
It was a BMW.
He tried to touch me.
'Don't,' I said. 'I've got a tampax in.'
But I wanted him.
His words were pure love,
'I don't mind,' he said.
My mascara had run.
I should have gone home.

Not everything was destroyed.
That was worse.
The sold the damage.
Salvaging charred dresses, odd shoes,
scalded mannequins.

Everything rained on.
Shawn chewed chewing gum.
So did I.

I looked at faces differently.
Daddy was quiet for a long time.

PRIVATE LOVE

Becoming a lesbian gave me a voice
And took away my tongue.

I am a professional lady –
Acceptable;
I am a predatory pervert –
Shocking;
Efficient, disruptive, reliable, abnormal –
I introduce clients,
I seduce women.

By day I wear a dress
Coolly answer telephones.
I sleep rough at night
Hot in another's bed.

My lover knows hard wisdom
Learnt from silences in public,
Where unsettled voices
Piss abuse –
'What d'ya call that, mate?
Is it a girl, or a geezer?'

'At times like this,' she says
'I wish I had a submachine gun.'

I watch my quiet and beautiful terrorist
Despised, pick herself up
Become a woman again.

Our private love trembles to be enough
Where no rituals reward our desire;
Shy and weary we battle
For how we are
And map out shorter, safer routes
Through forbidden territories
Which grow large,
More dangerous.

Yet before us pass proud lovers
Who will still come,
Will grace our sheets
Move wet for our touch.
Their renascent hopes
Crowd our rooms –
They strengthen me.

For now we hold fast and fierce to love
Beyond the cry of early passion,
It hurts to catch the heart
On sharp, unfinished compromise.

A REAL PHONE

I want a real phone.
A big square one
that rings through the house,
not a trim oblong
of a phone that shrills.

I want a round dial
that spins slowly
through the numbers
making long distance
seem very far away.
Not easy fingertip
buttons that beep
connections instantly.

I want a real phone
one with a receiver
that I can hang up
if I need to,
not a phone that you set down
when finished.
There's no finality to that.
No abrupt tring.
No satisfying statement.

I want a real phone.

REBECCA SWIFT

REBECCA SWIFT had several poems published in *Amazon* magazine while she was at Oxford University reading English. Since then, she has worked as a freelance TV researcher, journalist and is currently in publishing. She has recently edited *Letters from Margaret: A Correspondence Between Margaret Wheeler and Bernard Shaw 1944-1950* (Chatto & Windus, 1992).

ON REMEMBERING GETTING INTO BED WITH GRANDPARENTS

It's amazing we got that far, loveless,
As you were supposed to be, yet suddenly
I have a longing for your tripeish thigh;
Swallows, thronging to the eaves; a teasmade
Playing boring Sunday news and all sorts of
Rites and rituals which seemed noteable but
Were really just trips in and out of the
Bathroom, the neurotic pulling back of
Curtains, stained glass window at the top of
Hall stairs; dark chocolate like the secret
Meaning of the world in a corner cupboard:
Three-quarter circle smooth as a child's
Dreams and as far above reach . . .
'Loveless', the daughters said, years later when
The slow-lack peppered in their brains like a dust,
And life had grown as troublesome as thought.
Yet just tonight, I am dreaming of your thigh,
And of the unconscious swallows thronging to the eaves.

THE CONTRACT

The intermittent almost-hours decreed and
Squared affection like an old master. Love,
Spilt from the conversation like a milk and
Begged to be taken seriously, but there was
Nothing in the contract that was happy
With this. Salt recoiled up mothering ducts
And peculiar thoughts sprang up like wild flowers
Scattered, by the unaccountable mouths of birds

T.P. TOLKIEN

T. P. TOLKIEN was born in St. Louis, Missouri in 1962 and educated at Smith College and The Courtald Institute. Her work has appeared in various magazines. She lives in London and has a two-year-old son.

'About the Lady who Married Colonel Packard' was shortlisted for the 1992 Arvon Poetry Competition.

POMPEI

The impact broke her waters
flooding their neat linen bed
with a sea-like smell that clings
to certain bodily events.
So the twins felt that heaviness once
of life
but only at its end.
And all three slotted in
body within body
sealed in her room
like chinese boxes
of flesh and bone and stone.

They wait on the dark of earth
three strangers
steeping in quiet
stacked like leaves
from a book half written.
Rain falls
in their green church yard.

Until some distant hand
is sifting through the layers
and reveals them
carefully

whisking aside their dust
with a small technical brush.
He catalogues the way that bones
fall over time.

Like fitted stones shifting
slightly out of line
until one day a wall trembles
collapsing in the long grass
in which you can see
a woman upright, but not too tall.

Her sons curl like twin birds
one on each wing of her pelvis.
Their baby skulls are brittle
and they smile at each other
content as shepherds
surveying their flocks,
for the little jaw bones are smooth
they've tasted nothing
of what they have lost.

A FACE AT THE WINDOW

I think
they shot acid in my oranges.
The plumber might have pissed
in my bath.

The imagination spreads
like a carnation's
blood red lace.

It's scary out tonight.

ABOUT THE LADY WHO MARRIED COLONEL PACKARD

It appears that she is meditating on her sins
involving accounting procedures, the dinner menu
and a pet monkey that peed on the rug.

I

He settles back on his special chair
covered in dark green velveteen.
He's wrapped up tight in a slippery robe
with a satin belt and red lapels
that look like sword strokes
bleeding, crossing on his chest.

The fire has gone out of him at last.
So he calls the boy who lights his pipe
tidies up and pours the scotch.
Ice cubes clink in a crystal glass
and he growls a bit to clear the room
so the boy withdraws, apologising
bowing backward through the door.

This is Colonel Packard after his day
whipping natives, giving orders
'plowing through the chaos
of dimwitted, uncivilised minds'.
He's done his job well, he can relax
and for him this means the snap
of a spy novel opening.
He cracks its spine a little
across his knee.

II

She sits well back, occupies her corner
in a chair from the kitchen that is wooden
and hard. She reasons with her hands
begs them to be still.
But they do fidget and occasionally they jump.

Suddenly she feels his blue eyes pause
so she freezes like a deer hoping to disappear,
while his ears focus and sift the air.
He listens for mutiny, he fishes for sound.

She eludes him this time so he turns a page
and she breathes again but only with care.
She cannot afford to draw his attention
to meet his eye, sneeze or speak or stand
and pass with her back to this resting snake.

For small things, trigger him.

III

She wishes she were allowed a hobby.
It would be nice for her to sew,
leaning over like an angry swan
stitching, beating, expressing herself
to the face of a linen drum.

She might have been happy stabbing cloth
making it take her needle
from the back, from the front.
She could have had some purpose then,
an anchor for the wanderings of her hands.

They will not settle here. Her disobedient
hands. Lost in this heavy man's room.

IV

He sinks right back now
and his book settles on his heart,
like a field dressing on a major wound.
He reposes, dozing and his feet point
at the ceiling.

She imagines music
and flowers popping up all around him
lillies and orchids
and other dangerous looking varieties.
She inhales their funereal perfume.

He is wearing his black slippers
and it seems like he skinned a lot of small animals
to make shoes of their pelts.
She shivers at the whiteness of his foot
thinking how slippers can look so cruel against flesh.

V

Her hand goes to her throat, loosening
the high collar that she always wears.
It is hot here, but she hates her own flesh
the way that it was taken over, subdued
and marked.

People think she is merely modest
with her grandmother necklines, old fashion
puffed sleeves. She fastens so many pearl buttons
and they look like little baby teeth.

The sunglasses do spoil this image
but she does not wear them everyday
and so she tells herself
'this is not the world's end'.

VI

The world is him
in a pool of yellowing light.
He sleeps near the standard lamp
like he's sleeping under a mushroom
ragged with fringe. . .
And from this perspective
he is really not so very large.

The world seems like a photograph.

It is clocks ticking louder and louder.
(He is starting to snore now.)
(His ginger mustache shudders.)

The world is this room, this house
this garden, this district.

It is envelopes thudding on the mat.
Bills and magazines.
Letters from home.

ANXIETY

Shades are drawn against the London yellow night.
The fires are covered. All is closed.
The mad whirling wound down,
and somebody sleeping left the radio play.

If you raised a candle to this room.
If you brought a light to my heavy black element,
I would seem so calm.
A perfect specimen resting on a stone bed.
Cotton wound, sheeted, displayed in a church.

How can it move through a locked door?
Stealthy on feet like leaves.
It brushes the desk, the chair, the bed
as it passes.
I can smell its hothouse breath.

Rare and winding tendrils lift my dress.
They look beneath. Tease, touch
then shoot down and grip, curling on my ankle
snaking up my leg, tight.

Cattleprod fingers fan out
across my breast then my throat.
This gigantic hand is sharp, it's skeletal
but it leaves no mark.

My skin responds, a bed of seedlings
maturing in a moment on time lapse film;
electrical, speeded up, blotting each other out,
reaching for the white hot oven of sun.

Fear comes and I wish I was dreaming.
It parts my curtain but makes no real sound.
Fear comes when the window blackens.
It walks alone on city streets.
No dragon. No demon. It is a creature
without face.

RUTH VALENTINE

RUTH VALENTINE has had many poems published in
magazines and anthologies and a pamphlet of her work,
The Identification of Species, is available from Slow Dancer
Press. She lives and works in London.

These poems have been included in *Critical Quarterly, Slow
Dancer, The Rialto* and *Orbis*.

VARIATIONS ON A THEME OF CHARDIN

like wanting to photograph light itself:

not as it falls across an upholstered chair,
a book, a dusty window,

but peeled intact off surfaces
as a child floats a faded stamp
tenderly off its scrap of blue paper

or as you walk through lone
nectarine evenings

the print of his hand still watermarks your spine

AT SELSEY

Then climbing a breakwater at low tide, I found it again:
the sharp smell in the green
weed, the smell of life in the inchdeep pools,
the limpets pricking my feet, a soft
handslip on bladderwack   my eyes

opened. There were the coiled
threads left by the worms, there were mussel-shells,
the sand patterned with water, hard
and giving, the waves licked at my feet,
the beach in the evening light was blue and dun

And then I saw them there, my lost maligned
old women: walking the sand
in coats, in strong black shoes, with firm
slow steps, as they'd always been
and I'd forgotten.   This was their place and they'd come

to find them, not knowing it but looking
all day in the hidden churchyard by the lagoon.
They walked with the sun behind them, they were dark
to my eyes, I could not see
either one's face   I knew they were not smiling

but content perhaps, the rhythm of water and the sea
stilled them at last. And then
the wet sand wove the sky in its paisley-patterns,
the air was cold, I sat down
on a breakwater, some children

called from the clay-sand puddles   and they'd gone
back to the grass and the stone they came from.
I was orphaned again on the calm
dun and blue beach   the brown
pebbles   the old rasp of the sea, the wind

cold on my feet. I narrowed my eyes to the sun,
a dog ran to the water, boys
dug in the sand for worms, and there was no-one
like them, no old determined women
with a stick, a hat, a dearth of words

walking away or towards me. I wanted to keep them
but the tide turned in and the sun
lay pale on the water, one
hoarse seagull rose   in the mist
the tenuous island   billowed the horizon.

JENNY VUGLAR

JENNY VUGLAR is a New Zealander who has lived in
London since 1979. She has been a member of a women's
writing group since the summer of 1981. She has been
published in various magazines and anthologies and was a
prize winner in the 1989 Arvon Poetry Competition with
the poem 'Daughter: Post Operative.'

'Daughter: Post Operative' was published in the Arvon
International Competition 1989 Anthology; 'Daughter:
13th Birthday' in Writing Women Vol. 8, No. 1; and
'40 Weeks' in *Writing Women*, Vol. 9, No. 1.

DAUGHTER: POST OPERATIVE

I

Just now everything is still and white,
snow, or the light on snow.
If hills could breathe they would breathe like this
heavily, laboured; full of rocks and earth.
In this country we would all be lost
the creases and folds
are no whiter than your arms;
there are no landmarks
south of the thin line of your lashes,
dark as coal seams,
still as an airless day.
Only this breath moves
misting the oxygen mask
wrenching apart mountains.

II

Today there are shadows
as though the light hits at an angle;

along your wrist
and on the inside of an elbow
the skin is darkening.
The hospital gown has slipped from one shoulder,
inside violence purrs;
blood dried to a smear,
the caustic of sterilants.
Outside it could still be snow
but we can hear the beasts prowling.

III
Blood is the darkest colour,
night blackens it
but by day it glowers:
the unspeakable eyes that loom in caverns,
the dull glow of lanterns
carried by hobgoblins,
tarnished rubies,
pebbles drying as the sea ebbs.

This is a dark river
that flows into secret places;
under the ice
everything is burning.

IV
A day has passed
but there is no day here.
Light is unchanging, bleak
and merciless.
The northern lights play
constantly; cold, distant,
moving colours
on the inside of eyelids.

Tides sweep in seconds
sucked from one side of a tube

to the other.
There is no moon,
only the hollowed crescent
of your chest,
breathing unwillingly,
pulling at oceans.

V

Machines are crawling
caterpillar tracks criss cross;
there are sheets of paper flying in the wind.
Atoms are breaking
but in this great space
words have become another language
there are no stones to decipher.

This is a world learnt on fingers
with gestures and mistakes.
Alarms and each attendant panic
become lessons in lettering –
this number is oxygen, dropping;
this stroke above a line
a temperature too high.

This is the white of the enemy
that I can only stare into.

VI

There is a moth struggling
the quick beat beat
of tattered wings;
There is the shallow rattle
of water running over dry stones;
but more than this
I am afraid of silence.
Nothing is singing.

VII

This blue is not the blue of sky
or if it was, it has thickened,
crossed into cloud, but still blue;
blue as the estuary after rain
waters stiff with silt or a high
tide in the bay, waves heavy with sand.
Blue and something else that drags
and whimpers; not the blue of sky.

These eyes rolled dull like ageing
arum lillies, like last week's flowers.
I have nothing to add.
This blue I have shut eyes on.

VIII

Suddenly the land is turning
the flat waste clears
and where cloud
pulled the distance tight
a space is beckoning.
This is the horizon where
the earth rounds into the sun.
We are breathing without masks
sucking air straight
from the greening
of each black branch.
Your eyes are bright with pain
dark as blackbirds warbling,
the throat of them!
the throat of them!

40 WEEKS

I am beginning to hide beneath stones
to pull straw out of crevices,
hold testing fingers into wind.
These cold days have huddled fat about me
mud settles around my eyebrows
and I am wading through thick air
with you settling between my legs
like a boulder, an erratic
left on the edge of thawing.

This time lies sleeping
an automaton wipes dishes
carries shopping in strange bags
I have become a dinosaur
lumbering towards extinction.
Only the skin, tough and heavy,
the teeth jagged as nights
broken into fragments,
these things
the small sea I carry in each cell
the rough dolphin that bucks water
these things
and my teeth that tear apart words
bury everything under this tangle
of tired bones and long days
that turn and twist like smoke in wind
old leaves, slumber,
and then that fierce burning.

TO A DAUGHTER ON HER 13TH BIRTHDAY

May was there a damp affair
between contractions I could hear the plumbers
tramping up and down the hall
unblocking drains, sweeping sewage
off the back lawn.
Afterwards the veranda
flapped with nappies all winter.

Before that I remember
watching rain sweep up the bay
you rippling my skin like wind on water.

At your birth I was delivered,
made over, given a new name.
For weeks I woke on sheets
that clung to my breasts
wet as a baptism.

May on this side of the world
is still moist
but winter is behind us.

Paper table cloths swing like Jacob's
cloak against long grass. The fatted
calf has turned bright with cake.
Candles are burning but this year
more than years, I celebrate you here
and not, as I thought in March
when your heart jackhammered your chest,
dead.

That bereavement has no word;
not widow, relict, just un mothered.
From this wet may to something
arid; sand, dust, a dry wind
and the day roofless.

Jackie Wills

JACKIE WILLS was born in 1955. She has been widely
published in poetry magazines over the past six years. She
works as a freelance journalist and helps organise poetry
readings and workshops in Brighton where she lives with
her son and partner.

Her poetry has appeared in *Wide Skirt, Slow Dancer, Verse,
Honest Ulsterman, Poetry Wales* and *The Rialto*. A pamphlet,
Black Slingbacks (1992), was published by Slow Dancer Press.

HAT TRICK

The fortune teller sweats
as she speeds through her commentary
picking out prizes
the way I used to dip hands
into sawdust at village fetes
for a pistol or warped plastic mirror.
This time it's twins and confetti.
I went for the hat trick,
cards, palm and crystal ball.
But later, comparing notes,
find my future's the same as Jane's.

So I drive to the pool
left behind by quarrymen
where trees have no reflections.
There could be carp below the leaves.
I imagine them moving slowly over mud.
Water fills vacuums faster than air
in this damp country.
No-one would dare fish here.

OUT OF BOUNDS

Those pew chairs were rigid,
screwed together tight with batons –
you'd pull backwards, push forwards
but would never separate yourself
from that row of bowed heads.

If we could, we'd skive
to caves among the rhododendrons
and below their pink and purple balloons
read the Thoughts of Chairman Mao
or a dog-eared issue of Cosmo
with its famous full length male nude,
listening for the Geography master with his cane.

When it was safe,
we'd sneak into the nun's graveyard,
ringed with roses and horse chestnuts,
reddening the grass around them.
It was out of bounds, taboo
as the lipstick we saw a Sister trying
in an upstairs window,
maybe because she just wanted
some colour on her face, to be surprised
when she checked her veil in the mirror.

THE ROPEMAKERS

After stooping through a tunnel washed smooth by floods
our guide switches off the lights and we stand
still as stalagmites trying to guess where he is
from the strength of his sweet, beery breath telling us,
as if he's engineered it himself, there'll never be a crack
of sun or moon in here – where each winter three rivers
once collided and tons of water was forced upwards,
pummelling a ceiling more intricate than any stately home's.
Above, near the entrance, the ropemakers
lived – twisting and plaiting – and after rain or thaws,
had no need of ears, just mouthed and lipread
above the roar, their faces yellow in the candle flames,
paled by daylight only a few hours a week.

The old Anglia can't take it and my parents' plans for driving
through the night give out with the engine in a sheet of rain.
By fluke my father finds a garage, a removals van
filling up, so we're lifted, floppy with tiredness,
into the back to lie on blankets in the dark. No signposts,
no blinding headlights for my father to swear at
when they won't dip, no orange glare at each new town –
just that rattle of a toolbox and roll down door.
They could be taking us anywhere.
My mother promises tomorrow she'll pick us cherries.
My brothers whisper themselves to sleep, but I know
why the ropemakers avoided that hole in the back
of their cave, so opaque, immune to wax and matches –
it could draw you in by accident,
commanding silence while skin slowly covered your eyes.

JAPONICA

Our house shuddered with basslines
as my brother burst into his teens
like a skinhead emerging from a chrysalis.
Downstairs, watching tv, we'd feel the room vibrate –
dialogue drowned out as his filled with sound,
thick as the smoke from my father's non-stop cigarettes.
No-one dared knock on his locked door
we just turned the volume up,
until it became a duel and when each record stopped
we'd rush for the set, ashamed to be caught out.
It could go on for hours until he went for a bath,
every towel left wet as a flannel on the floor.
When he came out, his face had been picked
into a mess of blotches and blood.

But he was the only one of us who knew the latin names
of plants at ten, who'd asked for a patch of his own
in the garden, where he planted lettuce alongside daffodils
and night scented stock. He buried japonica apples
all along the fence one day because the pink flowers
were my mother's favourites. He took the dog
on a five mile walk across the common
the day it was put down and he knew why my father
had spent so many months at home
but never let on – just punched more holes
in each cheap plywood door.

BRIAR WOOD

BRIAR WOOD was born in 1958 in Tamarunui, New
Zealand and grew up in Auckland. She was editor of the
poetry section of *City Limits* magazine for two years and
lectures at the University of North London in Creative
Writing and New Literature in English.

GIRL FROM MARS TELLS OF MARVELS

Chosen out of thirteen thousand hopefuls
Britain's first astronaut, Ms Sharman,
used to be a confectionery scientist.

She described the practical difficulties
encountered in her eight day mission
to the Soviet station Mir. Sleeping

on her head or feet. Putting on socks
with both hands holding her down.
Just one foot as anchor. An orange glow

on re-entering earth's atmosphere. Force
breathing. I could see the surface
of the spacecraft melting. The sudden

burst of weightlessness. The majestic
power of the launch. Team spirit.
I hope the voyage has fuelled the debate

for future co-operation, government
to government. Increased awareness of
the preciousness of our planet.

About founding a women's astronaut club –
I would not join if such a club existed.
There is very little difference

between men and women in space.

IMPEDIMENTS

Never go overboard for a poet.
Shady characters. Preening with peacock
eyes at the back of their heads.
Poets live on extended credit

and are not habitually insured against
third party, spontaneous combustion, theft.
Poets are gobsmacked by statistics.
K.O'd. Red granite stumbling blocks

such as the clench of Amenophis III
gripping its fistful of documents.
They catnap all day and walk by night.
Especially the ones with come to bed

looks might pull the wool over your eyes.
They make you stay on their leyline,
haul you squalling into their orbit.
You never get to sleep with poets –

those piss artists. They rub your
nose in meaningful conversation.
Even the ones who will not touch
a drop of alcohol, instantaneously

corner you with Ancient Mariner gaze.
And as for the company they keep –
such friends. With domino principles.
Chequered careers. Attention spans

of a nanosecond and the life cycle
of a fruitfly. Unbridled liars –
do not expect a poet to know why.
No oil paintings, they have migraine

dispositions. Lenders, borrowers,
dinner parties where everybody gets along
like a house on fire. Poets and Co.
know how to make a crisis out of

a psychodrama. Inadequate as hosts
at a crunch, permanently out to lunch.
Poets are well known kleptomaniacs,
snatching the words out of your mouth,

whisking a shirt off your back.
Lightfingered. Casing a joint the moment
we walk into it. Gauntlets of small talk.
Poets survive in the nick of time.

ANGELS TREAD

It was reported in the Guardian, *by Virginia Vargas, that on Feb 15th, 1992, Maria Elena Moyano, ex-president of the Federation of Popular Women (VES) in Peru, was machine gunned to death. She was killed by a Sendero Luminoso group while taking part in fund raising activities for the VES as her children and other women watched. Then her body was blown up with dynamite.*

Could it have been the Ecstasy
we did not take the evening before?
Morning went treading on eggshells
slithering backwards over snow.

Marble writhed with ivy
between the plots at Highgate –
vibrant silence. Stone seraphims
blowing trumpets of their own.

To have tried to believe in
the miracle of bi-location.
Once on Oxford Street I was
counting sheep, sleeptalking,

saw grandfather's lanoline hands
overheard a long dead uncle chuckle
tickling his daughter's chin
with a wand of pussy willow

and point to a spawl of clematis
as if the Milky Way just landed
entangled in the angle of trees.
Breathed in the sharpness,

the virescence of sheep dung
catching the tube on Bond St.
Bit into a whitebait fritter
by the grave of the patriarch

Karl Marx. A red carnation army.
Chrysanthemums for Radclyffe Hall.
Rank roses and lily stiff poses
at the Rossetti family slab.

Isabel said 'What if . . .
Maria Moyano, for example . . .'
Synchronising lives. Meanwhile
the hoverfall of a feather

just in front of us, the path
split and some lovers kissed
in the fling of spring, held
hands with sycamore wings.

SHOPPING FOR SEX

So we go to Anne Summers
closing down sale – a scruffy
crew with money scorching
a hole in our pockets.

The branch manager,
an ageing Jo'burg queen
tells me he'll never go back
to South Africa.

He finds my passion for
New Zealand very strange.
Speakers blare
Air on a G String.

Tony reads magazines
holding out centerfolds
as we debate over outfits
with tradenames like

Lola, Tracy and Roxanne.
Helen says it's risky –
that fabric makes you itchy.
Sam explains they won't

be on long enough
to cause a problem
and buys a Fury set –
shocking pink, in PVC.

The edible knickers
resemble cat gut but
he tosses them in the basket –
free, gives Sam a nurse's kit

complete with toy thermometer.
Just as we're about to leave
with crotchless knickers,
dildos combat jockstraps,

in a plain paper wrapping
he finds banana vibrators
and rushes up to us with one
proffered, batteries revving

like an outboard motor.

SACCHARINE DADDY

While mom earbashed me

on the drive home from Ronny Scott's
slumped drunk in a black cab
I remember you swayed to Nina Simone
humming *Put a Little Sugar in My Bowl*.

Jamming the baby grand –
you were a stake
against which I leaned,
unruly scarlet runner bean.

What a squat solid citizen.
Portly barrel you rattled on
in that soiled suede overcoat
and Joseph Stalin rasp.

Hate was too puling a word –
I tried to despise your blind adoration
for anything and everything American.
Barracuda through and through.

Chainsaw massacres took place
in the back seat of a family sedan
as you abused Sunday drivers,
face beaming like neon.

Agamemnon's death mask.
Pills and a diet
for high blood pressure.
No more pavlova.

All Papa Meilland heart,
red cabbage patches
and pandering to grandsons.

And then again just for the record

a Nat King Cole version of
Moonlight in Vermont
on Sunday evenings
as we kids riffed to sleep –

For All We Know

STRAWBERRY MORNINGS

Three abreast, arms linked,
backpedalling then whizzing
forward, a shaky circus act –
we'd row up Tidal Road

while a rusty sun trundled higher
into skies blue as a swimming pool.
Sour thirteen, each one of us
tart and smart with repartee.

The pay was dismally minimalist.
We fooled around too much
to make money but we had lives
affluent with fantasy.

Olga, lusting for a chemistry set,
Ingrid, wanting purple hot pants,
and a library of leather bound
classics. So literal, I just wished

for more books. And scarlet hot pants.
We lay in the hollows stuffing
our voluble mouths or smuggling
ripe ones down our T Shirts

where the nipples were supposed
to grow. We pelted each other
with rotton specimens or stuck
green ones up our noses to make

each other laugh. Then started
a competition over who could
find the biggest, scoff the most.
One day later Ingrid came out

in hives, I saw red lights
while Olga got fired
for distracting the customers,
blatant lane hopping and

squashing too much fruit.

ANN ZELL

ANN ZELL was born in 1933 in the United States, lived in
London for twenty years and has now settled in Belfast. She
has had poems published in *Poetry Ireland Review*, *The Honest
Ulsterman*, *The Salmon* and in an anthology of Irish women's
writing, *Women's Work*. She has one daughter.

'To Be A Grandmother' was published in *Krino* (Winter
92/93), 'Afterbirth' appeared in *The Honest Ulsterman*, and
'The Mind Retains' in *Poetry Ireland Review*.

AFTERBIRTH

It's not true I didn't want you.
I wanted you enough to give you room
in a space so small and undefined
it's a wonder we didn't both suffocate.

It's not true I didn't love you.
I loved you without invention
those months when you commandeered
all my reserves for your growing.

How was I to know,
in that life before you were born,
the child of the mind is a doll
to the child of the belly?

You were so new you were still evolving
when they left us alone together;
kicking the air like a stranded frog,
flexing fingers from which the web
had barely vanished; using your lungs
to pierce the shell of the world.

I had the means to ease your hunger,
but your cries foretold
pain I couldn't nullify,
cravings no dealer would satisfy

and after you slept
I sat in the dark, rocking
like a child taken too soon from her mother,
while love curled up in a hard white ball
and wouldn't come out for panic.

THE MIND RETAINS

A birthdate or an address close to mine,
the chance occurrence of a common name;
fragments of patient data recombine,
illusory kinship skews my reference frame.
The intimate statistics of an unseen
woman whose felt lump is identified
invade the necessary space between
recorder and malignance classified.

Cancer results are my reality.
I deal in findings, not in therapy.
Sending reports to clinics and to store,
holding essentials in the memory core.
My mind maintains a different history:
imagined women safe from surgery.

TO BE A GRANDMOTHER

Dreaming, she carries her daughter's unborn child
as an egg, warm in her armpit.
Awake, broody as an old hen,
she casts her concern onto a circular
needle, trying to lose herself in pattern.

The wool smells like the bottle-fed lambs
they kept warm in a box behind the stove –
milky and precarious –
and she's hooking her needle
through loops of memory.

The shortlived sister her mother named Joy.
The lambs raised to go
like themselves to the slaughter.
Her own grandmother, mythical with age
in a house that had forgotten children

as she has forgotten children, unsure
about renovations.
She awaits wisdom. She knows knitting.
In the middle of a difficult row
craft evens her tension.

Ribbed body, legs and arms
she fashions a spell for a winter baby,
each stitch a worked charm.
If her knitting has anything to do with it
this child will be one of the lucky ones.